The Exciting Life of Being a Woman : A handbook for women and girls

feminist webs

HAMMER/ON

Copyright

Published by Hammeron Press
www.hammeronpress.net

© Hammeron Press
All rights reserved
Printed and bound in United Kingdom
05 12
First Edition

251 p.cm

ISBN 978-0-95645-072-2

Editors
Amelia Lee and Debi Withers

Cover Design
Tamzin Forster

Layout/Illustration
Tamzin Forster

Contents
Created by members of Feminist Webs

Typefaces
3rd Man, Certto Headline, Baron
Kuffner by Bumbayo Font Fabrik
Keytabmetal by Tension Type,
Helvetica Neue by Max Miedinger
Handwriting Dakota by Altsys
Metamorphosis

This book has been made possible
due to a kind donation from the
Heritage Lottery Fund Young Roots
Programme

Contents page

Introduction – Beginning with us
Who we are and why we wrote this book

by Amelia Lee

We are a group of women. Women just like many of you reading this now. Some of us are young, some of us older, some disabled, some not. We come from difference races, places, religions, sexualities and classes. What brings us together is that we like being women. Women of all shapes and sizes and talents.

Once-upon-a-time each one of us started out a child and began to grow up, to become a woman, and to find out many wonderful things about the world.

But as we grew, each one of us began to get an unsettling feeling deep down inside that something in the world isn't quite right. That jokes about rape aren't funny. That being wolf-whistled at by strangers at night when you just want to walk the streets in peace is **not** ok. That other people trying to take control of your ideas, your confidence, your independence and your body is **BAD NEWS.**

So feeling this sense of unease, we began to look across the vast and wondrous world that we were finding out about, and started to talk to other women. We found out that many women shared ideas about the world with us. They had decided to make the world better for women: To challenge the bad things women experience, and to look at the bigger reasons why these things exist. These women are feminists. Their

Ideas generated by young women at Feminist Webs workshop

mission: to end sexism.

"Sexism
is the UNEQUAL power between genders. "

They were living the exciting life of being a woman. They were talking about society's old fashioned ideas about women, debating about women's bodies, about power, about life, and carving out a life for themselves that isn't about being a stereotype and IS about believing in yourself. We became like these women. We became feminists.

What is SEXISM?

- Power/control
- Discrimintaion
- Inequality
- Unfairness
- About gender
- Historical
- Always focused on women – says a lot!
- Glass ceiling – career ladder
- Humourous, eg. the butt of humour (small feet – nearer sink)

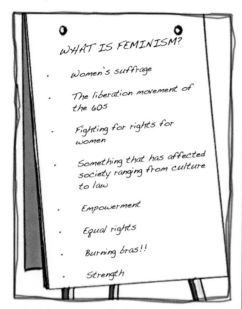

WHAT IS FEMINISM?

- Women's suffrage
- The liberation movement of the 60s
- Fighting for rights for women
- Something that has affected society ranging from culture to law
- Empowerment
- Equal rights
- Burning bras!!
- Strength

Ideas generated by young women at Feminist Webs workshop

But when we looked around, we couldn't find pictures of women like us on billboards, or on the television, in museums. Or in books or on the internet. 'Why is this exciting life so hidden?' we thought. 'Where can women (young and old) go to find out about their sisters throughout the world, about themselves, about this exciting life?'

And so we sought out and found such places, many places, that women had created: libraries, books, films, archives, pictures, music, gardens, safe spaces, clinics, protests, community centres, homes and conversations at tables in kitchens all over the world.

But these were often small groups of women, only loosely connected to one another. So we had an idea. What if each woman, each place, each idea could be connected? What exciting things might happen in our lives then? What if we spun a web to connect all these women together? And so, we did. We spun Feminist Webs. Because, in the wise words of the Ethiopian proverb,

"When

spiders unite they can tie up a lion.

"

Ethiopian Proverb

Feminist Webs is a movement of young women, youth workers and academics. We want to record and capture the best bits of youth work with girls and young women from the past, and use this knowledge to make a better world for young women in the future. We have created resources, booklets, a website, an archive, art, delivered many events and exhibits, and sparked lots of ideas in the women we meet. We are making history, or should that be herstory!? And with this book, we hope you will join us!

Photo by Jean Spence

Six or seven years ago,
in York train station,
two women found each other...

They both happened to be youth
workers with a shared passion
girls work in particular.

It occurred to them: Would
girl's work be forgotten
soon? What would happen
all the progress we've
made?

Perhaps a network ....a
WEB of women could
come together and create
an archive...

6

Shortly after a meeting was held, 35 women gathered together in Manchester to make an archive.

'They also decided to create a pack of resources for youth workers and women. They called this booklet 'done hair and nails, now what?' to challenge the idea that women were only interested in beauty.'

Comic strip by Hebe Phillips

How you might want to use this book How you might want to use this book

You can read this book on your own, dip in and out, read from cover to cover, go off and do more research on the topics that interest you. Pass the book on to friends if you think you are done with it or if you think they need it!

Or you can use the book to set up your own girl's group, women's group or even cross generational women's group. You can do this formally in a youth club or community centre, or informally with friends, or even just one friend. You could work through the chapters as a way to help you think about different ideas and issues. You can do this yourself, DIY! In that way you are already part of feminist

Meetings Planner

Meeting
Venue
Start   Finish
Attendees   FEMINIST WEBS   18ᵗʰ MARCH 2006

Agenda

11am Talk by Janet on French modern feminist movement "Ni Putes Ni Soumises"
Mixed movement
300,000 ppl marches. Anti ♀ only space.
Have a website you can translate into English ✓
Charismatic leader Fevra O'Hara.

2 Safe spaces - Y.P more at risk in their own homes
3   than outside + yet Safety is key
4   rather than - go are take + risks
5 Accreditation - why do we push ppl into
6   assessment in youth work when
7   some people get it twice via school + youth
8   club whilst others fail twice -
9 Risk Assessments - why do we have to jump thro'
10   hoops to even take a group on a trip.
Do we want to get rid of gender so people can do
any job they want, or to have equality
so that "women's work" is paid the
same as "men's work"?
Yes / No / Maybe cards for sex health

Notes from the second Feminist Webs annual gathering

There has always been a women's movement

Women who fight for their rights and for the rights of other women are feminists. Since time began there have always been women who have done this. They might not have used the word 'feminist' to describe themselves. So it is hard for us to talk about feminism 'beginning'. It is also difficult for us to talk about exactly what it means, because it means so many different things to different people, and it changes all the time.

Here are some examples to help you think about your feminism:

WHAT IS FEMINISM?

- A movement that believes in the equality of the sexes/genders

- A movement which strives for the abolition of patriarchy

- Equal opportunities

- Choices

- Greenham Common

- Women's liberation

- Equality

- Allowing women to become independent, have a voice and to be true to themselves

Ideas generated by young women at Feminist Webs workshop

"Feminism

is the radical notion that women are human beings. "

Cheris Kramerae, 1996

" I myself have never been able to find out precisely what feminism is: I only know that people call me a feminist whenever I express sentiments that differentiate me from a doormat. "

Rebecca West, 1913

" A feminist is anyone who recognizes the equality and full humanity of women and men. "

Gloria Steinem

Because

woman's work is underpaid or unpaid and what we look like is more important than what we do and if we get raped it is our fault and if we love women it's because we can't get a real man and if we expect community care for our family we are selfish and if we stand up for our rights we are loud and if we don't we are typical weak females and if we want to get married we are out to trap a man and if we don't we are unnatural and because we aren't deemed responsible enough to decide if, when and how we give birth we are feminists

Original text by Joyce Stevens 1975

14.03.2008.

Omena's Speech for the Launch

I am Omena Osivwemu, aged 14, from Manchester. Also known as Kimberley Osivwemu's middle daughter! I am from a mixed heritage background and see myself as a British mixed-race Nigerian. In no situation would I class myself as simply one thing! But at the moment I do class myself as a young feminist!

I'm going to begin by telling you about feminism and what it is to me; feminism is important to me as a young woman because it gives me the strength and determination to challenge what I see as wrong. But also to recognise what is wrong and shouldn't be accepted. So as a young woman, I can use that strength, support and knowledge to help other women and girls around me.

Feminism for me is again, having the will power and assertiveness to discuss and consider challenges and issues that I wouldn't have before I got involved, and then to go on to doing something about putting it right.

Women only spaces and opportunities, such as feminist webs, are important as they give women of all ages and cultures the opportunity to discuss issues, which in male presence they would perhaps not. Also to be able to relax, as they don't have to worry about being competitive or being in male presence and men's gaze. By being women only, it gives us women the chance to express ourselves, be ourselves and enjoy ourselves.

'Feministwebs' is a group made up of feminist women and girls of all ages, which continues to grow and always welcomes new comers. We spread the word of feminism and how it is a positive thing. Plus we spread awareness of the help and opportunities there is out there for women and girls.

So, I hope now I have informed you all briefly about feminism and feminist webs, from my perspective. I will continue with outlining the current project, of which we are all present for the launch.

The current archive project is a physical collection of documents, audio, interviews, videos, publicity from past projects and books, all focused on youth work with women and girls, from a feminist perspective. Creating this archive has been made possible thanks to the sponsorship of the National Lottery Heritage Fund's Young Roots programme; so a big and grateful thank you to them. The archive can be used as a resource for future projects and research. It's such a wonderful thing because it contains so many untold **herstories**, which will now be preserved for centuries. Well actually, the herstories were untold till now!!

Our website: www.feministwebs.com (all in lowercase) is an online version of the archive, including extra benefits such as photos and profiles, which is easily accessible with modern technology.

To conclude; does anyone have any questions?

Next steps- what we want to happen enxt with the project e.g. making a film, doing a roadshow with the archive...?Thank you all for your attention, enjoy the rest of your time here. Be sure to ask anyone of us if you have any enquiries, and I hope the work we have done so far interests you.

Speech at Rosa Fund launch in 2008 by Omena Osivwemu, scanned in from Feminist Webs archive

What is else is Feminism about?

By 30 young women from North West England on a residential trip 2011 and on a residential for Oral History Training in 2009

- Empowering
- Women
- Same equal rights as men
- Suffragettes
- Campaigning
- Feminism is empowering women and campaigning for equal rights as men
- About girls and how girls dress
- They say you have to be feminine and girly but girls have a mind of their own, they can have their own choice and their own different dress sense
- Judgments: tomboy, get bullied, 'dyke,' 'lesbian,' get singled out, not safe, 'slag' 'slut,' they are sleeping around and impress boys, "a dress is not a yes"
- Women standing up for themselves
- Anti-sexism
- Challenging women's roles
- Sexuality
- Equality
- Women's rights
- Equal pay
- Making sure women have a say and are heard
- Being yourself not what society wants / expects you to be
- Women having equal rights to be themselves (whatever that is)
- Fighting stereotyping
- Not being a man-hater
- Cope / being strong (periods, giving birth), housewife, mother, maternal
- Men and woman
- Equal rights for women
- Someone who believes in the empowerment of women
- Someone who campaigns for the rights of women
- Misunderstood word
- Equality
- Women's issues

- Women live for equal rights and not to be treated badly by men!!!
- Having status in society
- Appreciating women
- Anyone can understand the underpinning values
- Women's rights and choices
- Emancipation
- Being confident in yourself as a woman
- Feminism
- Women's rights
- What it means to be female?
- Being valued for who we are
- Feminism, strength
- Everyone who values women for who they are
- All women being treated like they deserve to be treated
- Gender equality
- Archive
- Information-sharing and make change happen
- Progress
- History
- Knowledge / understanding
- Impact
- Strength
- Feminism
- And all women deep down!
- Be proud and equal
- Feeling good about being a strong woman!
- Women are people too so we should be noticed!
- Stand up and be heard!
- Fighting stereotypes
- Fighting against sexism
- Fighting for a good cause
- Fighting oppression
- Women to be equal to men
- Strong women! Equality for women! Oh happy days
- Celebrating all women
- Stand up!! Speak up!!
- FREEDOM!

Photo from the launch of Feminist Webs, 2009

- Men can support women's equal rights, and sometimes they might be called feminists. Some people think that only women can be feminists, and that male supporters of equal gender rights should be called pro-feminist men

- Being a feminist doesn't make you a lesbian any more than standing in a garage makes you a car! If you are not a lesbian, then joining a group for equal rights won't change you

- People wrongly associate feminists with 'burning bras'. There is little evidence to suggest anyone burnt bras as a protest. In the 1968 protest outside the Miss America competition, people threw lots of stereotypical women's clothes into rubbish bins, and this symbol became quite famous. In the 1960s, American men who refused to go to war in Vietnam did burn their draft cards as a symbol of their anti-war protest. So it is possible that people have confused these as the years have gone on

- Feminism isn't about 'women's issues' because what people call 'women's' issues are everyone's issues. Is parenting and childcare only women's responsibility, or should all genders be responsible? By re-thinking how we share out roles, men's lives also improve because they can live free from gendered stereotypes

So what does feminism look like?

t means women having as much freedom as men, including being able to walk the streets home at night without fear. It means that women have the knowledge and the resources to make informed decisions about their lives. You can choose to be an astronaut or a full-time stay-at-home parent or something completely different. You can choose when and if you have children. You can choose what you wear and when you wear it. Social equality also includes sportswomen being paid the same amount as men, and not having to take their clothes off to get on TV!

Illustration by Jackie Fleming

Feminism means having political equality with men. It means having a society where women are fully involved in politics and public life.

It means economic equality. On average, for every £1 a man earns in the UK in 2011, a woman earns 87.5p for doing exactly the same job!

Globally less than 5% of the world's property is owned by women. In many countries girls do not get the chance to go to school, so are denied opportunities to get an education which would lead to earning higher wages.

People call feminism an "ideology," which means it involves re-looking andt re-thinking about everything in your life.

What do you think? Taken from *The Him Book* by Chris Meade

	AGREE STRONGLY	AGREE	DON"T KNOW	DISAGREE	DISAGREE STRONGLY
'Women are naturally weaker than men.'					
'Men shouldn't have to cook their own meals.'					
'Women make better nurses than men.'					
'Women make better computer programers than men.'					
'Married women shouldn't go to work.'					
'Pictures of naked women in magazines are offensive.'					
'Women secretly encourage men to rape them.'					
'A woman should save herself for her husband.'					
'A man shouldn't cry.'					
'It's unnatural to love someone of the same sex.'					
'24 hour childcare should be available to everyone.'					
'Contraception is the women's responsibilty.'					
'Married women should be able to claim their own social security benefits.'					
'A man should always be offered a job before a woman.'					
'Women have the right to choose about abortion.'					
'Women have no right to have good jobs - they only leave to have babies.'					
'Men can't look after babies.'					

Thinking about feminist movements in waves
by Lucy Russell YWCA

Some people talk about certain times in Feminist History where there was a big movement or push, and they call these 'waves'. Not everyone agrees with this way of thinking about feminism, because the 'waves' happen at different times depending which country you are in. If you think only about the 'waves' you might miss everything important that happens in between. If you read more on feminism you will come across the term 'waves' so we have done a brief example of these here.

First wave feminism

The 'first wave of feminism' in the UK addressed how politics and the law discriminated against women. It looked at women's rights in work, voting, marriage and education. Most people think of this wave as being from the 1900s up to the Second World War (1939), but there was a long history before then of women demanding their rights.

In 1792 **Mary Wollstonecraft** published *A Vindication of the Rights of Women* calling for education for women and arguing that women are human beings who deserved the same fundamental rights as men.

In 1851 American **Sojourner Truth** spoke up about the experience of being a black woman in slavery and how different that was from being a white woman.

"That man over there says that women need to be helped into carriages, and lifted over ditches. Nobody ever helps me into carriages, or over mud-puddles! And ain't I a woman? I have ploughed and planted and no man could head me! And ain't I a woman? I could work as much and eat as much as a man - and bear the lash as well! And ain't I a woman?"

Sojourner Truth

The Suffragettes were groups of women who campaigned for women's rights to vote. They often used 'direct action' to do this. Before their campaign women had little political voice.

Direct action is activity undertaken by individuals, groups, or governments to achieve political, economic, or social goals outside of constitutional social/ political channels. For suffragettes this included chaining themselves to railings, and smashing windows, going on hunger strike, and putting bombs in post boxes.

It was not just the work of the Suffragettes that brought about change. The First and Second World Wars had a dramatic effect on women's roles in society, as they had to take on what had traditionally been men's jobs.

In 1918 women over 30 got the right to vote, and in 1928 women over 21 got voting rights.

Second wave feminism

'Second wave' feminism took place in the USA from the late 1950s onward. In the UK we had the Women's Liberation Movement, which was very active in the 1970s and 1980s.

This was the next stage on from basic legal rights, and looked at wider culture to see where there were problems. This included:

- looking at women's rights around motherhood and abortion
- the right to do 'non-traditional' jobs for women e.g. construction or engineering
- the right to be free from sexual violence
- looking at how language re-enforces sexism
- looking at how religion and other powerful groups in society have 'policed' women's roles

A famous phrase from this era is *'the personal is political'* by Carol Hanisch. This means that our interpersonal interactions, our culture, and decisions that affect our bodies, htomes and relationships, are as political, and are as much a part of discrimination as institutional discrimination, i.e. our right to vote.

Patriarchy :

The Women's Liberation Movement highlighted patriarchy as the root cause of women's disadvantage. Patriarchy is male power and dominance throughout our world. It is in obvious things like discriminatory laws and practices, in our prejudices like stereotypes and in discrimination. But it is also in customs, in our language and in our beliefs. It can be invisible and ingrained and difficult to identify and challenge.

As feminism developed, different groups of women found that their voices were not necessarily being heard. This lead to new and diverse threads of feminism developing to represent different groups or political views:

- Radical feminism
- Socialist/Marxist feminism
- Lesbian feminism (sometimes now grouped together Queer movement)
- Black and Asian women's feminism
- Sex-positive feminists
- Liberal feminists
- Individualist feminists
- Separatist feminists
- Ecofeminists
- Postmodern feminists
- Post-colonial feminists
- Religious feminists (e.g. Muslim, Jewish and Christian)

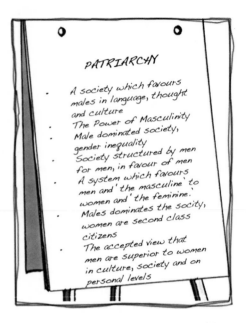

PATRIARCHY

- A society which favours males in language, thought and culture
- The Power of Masculinity Male dominated society, gender inequality
- Society structured by men for men, in favour of men
- A system which favours men and 'the masculine' to women and 'the feminine.'
- Males dominates the socity, women are second class citizens
- The accepted view that men are superior to women in culture, society and on personal levels

Ideas from Feminist Webs workshop

During the second wave there were some topics that received a lot of attention. Here are two in particular:

Pornography :

Some women saw pornography as objectification of women. That means women's bodies were turned into objects, rather than people. They saw pornography as an abuse of women and made a direct link between the portrayal of women as sexual objects and male-on-female violence. Other 'sex-positive' women believed that women were able to be more in control of their bodies and identities through sex.

Reproductive rights :

These are rights to contraception (e.g. 'The Pill'), abortion, to make decisions about your body and rights concerning motherhood. Feminists questioned why men, such as doctors, religious leaders or family and community leaders got to make the decisions about what happened to women's bodies. Women wanted power over their own bodies. Find out more about this in our *'Banged Up'* chapter.

Do we have a third wave of feminism?

Many feminists today are still looking at the same issues as women have always faced. We now see more clearly the differences in experience of women from all over the world, from a variety of races and backgrounds. Feminism should not be only about white, straight, able-bodied, middle class women from the USA and Europe. Feminism is for **ALL** women.

Donated to Feminist Webs archive from Girls work Resource Unit, Lancashire Youth and Community Service

Post-colonial feminism

Throughout history countries (e.g Britain) have invaded and controlled other countries. Sometimes this has been to steal the resources that country has, or to steal people as slaves. Many countries in Europe have done this to other countries, 'colonised' them. Even now, when many countries are independent again, the impact of being a colony is still very real.

Post-colonial feminism is about women who live in a culture that experienced colonisation from Western Europe or America. They argue that their experience is very different to that of first and second wave feminists. They explain that colonisation has had a dramatic impact on their culture. One of the effects is that the culture of the colonisers is often seen as better and is dominant, over their own experience. They call on feminism to reject these patterns of power and listen to the very diverse experiences of women. They say that oppressions relating to the colonial experience, particularly racial, class, and ethnic oppressions, have marginalised women in post-colonial societies. They also object to the stereotypyed portrayal of women in non-Western societies as passive and voiceless victims, as opposed to the portrayal of Western women as modern, educated and empowered.

Empowered sister activity

Take out a pen and fill in a word or phrase next to each letter that describes what feminism means to you.

F

E

M

I

N

I

S

M

RECLAIM

WOMEN'S MANIFESTO

- Respect yourself.
- Don't be a stereotype, do something useful with your life.
- Step up to challenges and back down from confrontations.
- Live by the positives rather than the negatives.
- You can learn a lesson from anyone, young or old.
- It's not where you come from, it's where you're going.
- Don't let brick walls stand in your way.
- 'I can't' is just another way to say 'I won't'.

Work as one and RECLAIM our area.

If you support our ideas, please display this in your window.

Thank you

RECLAIM is a project for 12-14 year old girls from 6 different schools in South Manchester. This manifesto shows their priorities, for their communities, in their own words.

Manifesto created by the young people of Reclaim - www.reclaimproject.org.uk

Chapter 1 - Resilience
(That means being strong!)

We have been talking about women: About the best things in our lives and the biggest challenges or threats to us. And we keep coming back to one word - resilience. Resilience being safe, having rights over our own bodies, having freedom in the work we do, deciding whether and how to have children. Resilience is always at the heart of who we are.

In 2011 we went on a two-day trip with women of all ages to explore the theme 'Women are Strong.' We did a number of activities and had lots of discussions. The result of these discussions you will find throughout this book.

Resilience - noun

1. The ability to bounce back, to be buoyant

2. To be able to return to your natural position e.g. after being squashed

3. The positive capacity to cope with stress or adversity. A process you can learn, rather than a personality trait.

Women's Self Defence

The Courage To Be Me!

Donated to Feminist Webs archive from Girls work Resource Unit, Lancashire Youth and Community Service

Wheel of Resilience:
Courtesy of www.healthedco.com

What resilience means to us

Taken from list we came up with on the residential trip 'Women are Strong' in 2011. Do you agree with us?

- 'Don't let the b......s grind you down'
- Coping and learning from experience
- Not letting anyone walk all over you
- Getting across what you think is right!
- Strength
- Courage
- Over-coming barriers
- Standing up for what is right
- The strength and courage of overcoming barriers that might stop you doing what you want to or being who you want to be
- Bounce back
- Strength to overcome oppression
- Working together
- Getting on with it!
- It's like a stress ball, you squeeze it but it returns to its original shape
- Being strong / able to cope
- Cope in different ways
- Strength in women's ways e.g. endurance during your period or childbirth
- Timing
- Escape
- Release co-operation between women
- Being different
- Different view points
- Understanding
- Coping strategies
- Being open-minded
- Empathy with others
- Support networks
- Independence
- Reflection
- Get female MPs to bring up important issues for women in Council and Parliament
- Protest – Reclaim the Night, Million Women Rise Marches
- Setting up women's community groups – support existing women's refuges (safe houses from domestic abuse) and set up more

From Lancashire County Council's Youth and Community Service. Donated to the Feminist Webs archive by Kate Clements.

This is our group time line of resilience in our lives...

We came up with this timeline as a group, looking at our own histories and how these connected to all women's history.

Pre-historic

- Women were owned – we were property
- Surviving & raising children
- Family came to UK, came out of slavery & became British citizens
- Grandma & aunts were nurses
- Strong woman in my family were disempowered following marriage – e.g. great grandmother!!
- My grandparents met each other, one Irish catholic, one Welsh/Irish protestant

Up to 20 years ago

- Volunteering abroad in Africa
- Listening to family talks
- Joined protest against NATO in Brussels
- Getting over a trauma
- Moved away from domestic abuse – fresh start – rethinking the important things
- I discovered yoga & that helps me look after myself
- Overcoming bullying at school
- I became a vegetarian, as a way of looking after myself & stopping cruelty to animals
- Visited miners' wives who supported their husbands on strike
- Starting girls groups & young women realised that they do have a voice
- Got into trouble & fights in school as I couldn't cope in that school. 5 years later I have settled down in a different school & got great grades -A*s & 5As!
- My mum left us so we had to fend for ourselves

Last year

- Still part of community owned, volunteer-run, hydro power company!
- Parents pressuring me but being able to make my own decisions & overcoming some fears
- Love
- Ending unhealthy things
- 'Slut walk' protest
- Being used, then bouncing back & staying strong
- Being academic to help run a course
- New friends came into my life
- Stated training doing something I want to do
- Performing at Manchester Pride
- Helped clear up the streets after the Manchester Riots
- Had to re-apply for my job
- Started new course so that I could change career direction – resilience to redundancy
- Finding and joining the Lik:t group at LGYM (a young lesbian and bisexual women's group)
- Got more involved with community & others!

Last year continued...

- After assaults & struggles within myself, I finally learnt to accept I am a woman & I am going to do well. Became happier within myself with my brown skin, mad hair & body shape
- Demonstrated at Chertsey with Campaign Against Arms Trade
- Moving away from home
- Joined an allotment
- I started high school
- Living independently – learning on my own
- My Nan told me to live for the moment and enjoy life!!
- About 2 years ago I started my career. Set up parents co-op, looked after sick relatives youth project in Longsight
- Defeating homophobia at home and school
- Learning to cope with retirement & finding new things to do & new people to meet with
- Went back to work after being off ill for over a year
- Leaving home made me a stronger person (standing up to parents)
- Being able to do courses & complete them
- Heart break!
- Starting a new job
- Identifying as a feminist
- Being given opportunities to gain knowledge that with possible future careers/plans helps
- Finding people who believe in me

Today

- Love my course – looking to a new direction in my life
- Coming to meet the Feminist Webs group
- New relationship
- Having big discussions
- Involvement with Feminist Webs is invigorating
- Being called stupid & proving everyone wrong with great GCSE results
- Active reflection working with Feminist Webs
- Coming here to Feminist Webs
- Continuing in fight for equal pay
- I have a youth club which allows me to be myself & gives me opportunities & support
- Getting girls & women out doing more things (not just sat at home)
- We speak about who we are, we talk, woman talk
- Be able to survive financially & mentally
- Friends
- Learnt new things

...and where we think there has been women's resilience in the wider world

The Past

- Surviving bubonic plague
- Resistance to Colonialism – British India, Africa, Caribbean
- World War 1 and 11 – women proved that they could look after themselves & undertook predominantly 'male' roles e.g. delivered spitfires & hurricanes to airports
- The fight for the vote and then Suffragettes getting the vote
- Opening of first refuges for domestic violence
- Mary Poppins brought the ideas of votes for women to a younger audience
- The pill was invented
- Sex Discrimination Act
- Gay Pride!!
- Gained rights as human beings. We began to assert our human rights
- Women in slavery narratives & novels being published to share their experiences

Recent history

- We organised around ideas of beingness, safety, identity, security
- 9/11
- More men attempting to share duties as parents & at home so more women can work full-time & follow careers
- Section 28 banning 'promotion of homosexuality in schools' is finally repealed
- Acknowledgment that rape can happen in relationships (male & female) & within same sex couples
- Lesbian, gay, bisexual and trans support groups start up
- Global social justice
- 2005 – civil partnerships rights
- Reclaim the Night, & Million Women Rise Marches and The Slut Walk
- Young Asian girls being able to do what they want & attend youth group
- Asian & white young people coming together
- Giving young people a voice & empowerment to change
- Organisations helping young women with problems
- Endangered Species International Body Image Summits
- Ken Clark speaks about sentencing for rape & sexual offences
- Sustainability - an even more important issue – particularly fuel poverty and global food issues
- Manchester bomb
- More women in parliament

These are some ways we want resilience to impact on our future:

- Next year I will run my own street dance classes around Manchester
- More active campaigning in school for women's rights
- The lesbian and bisexual women's cycling projects
- Going to university
- Being refused a job but constantly applying & trying
- Becoming an adult volunteer at my youth group
- To be clever
- To grow up brave
- 2013 I will go to Oxford or Birmingham University? Then I will start my journey to becoming an inspirational head teacher, helping deprived children achieve
- 2012 I will finish my book & publish it!!
- To be in my home! Finishing university & becoming a youth worker
- To touch an elephant
- Be my own person & I do what I want to do!
- Global feminism movement makes great achievements
- Maintain the changes in our lives
- Equal love policy
- Happiness, health, empowerment & fulfilment for future generations!
- Keep talking! Woman-talk about our womanist futures
- Keep marching, organising, enabling, empowering!

 Why not create your own timeline of resilience?

Fill in the boxes on the next page with things that have happened in your life which have helped you to be strong.

Your History...

Pre-historic	Years ago	Last year	Today	The future

From Lancashire County Council's Youth and Community Service. Donated to the Feminist Webs archive by Kate Clements.

Whose resilience inspires us?

Dr Maggie Aderin-Pocock
Born 1968

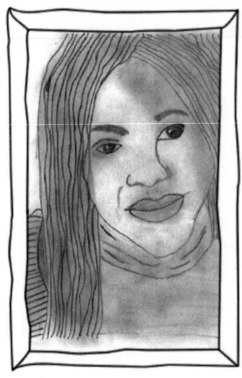

Space scientist and educator

Maggie was born in London to Nigerian parents. She has dyslexia. As a child she told a teacher she wanted to be an astronaut. It was suggested that instead she try nursing!

Maggie gained four A Levels in Maths, Physics, Chemistry and Biology. She went on to study at Imperial College London, where she graduated with a Bachelor of Science in Physics and a Doctorate in Mechanical Engineering.

Since gaining her doctorate, Maggie has worked on many projects, including private industry, government contracts and academic research.

Maggie is a pioneering figure in communicating science to the public, specifically school children. She engages children and adults all over the world with the wonders of space science. In her work Maggie is committed to inspiring new generations of astronauts, engineers and scientists.

In her career she has spoken to about 25,000 children, many of them at inner-city schools. She tells them how and why she is a scientist and is an inspiring role model to those that meet her.

In 2006 she was one of six 'Women of Outstanding Achievement' winners with GetSET Women. In 2009 she was awarded an MBE for her services to science and education.

Illustration by Harriet Gibson

Whose resilience inspires us?

Marie Curie was born Maria Salomea Skłodowska in Warsaw, in Russian Poland. She lived there until the age of twenty-four. In 1891 she followed her older sister Bronisława to study in Paris, where she earned her higher degrees at Sorbonne University.

In Paris she met her husband, Pierre Curie who was a Physics and Chemistry teacher at the Sorbonne. After Marie and Pierre married, the two physicists hardly ever left their laboratory. Marie had found love and a scientific collaborator who she trusted. In 1903 Pierre Curie, Marie Curie and Henri Becquerel were awarded the Nobel Prize in Physics for their discovery of radiation. In the same year Marie was awarded her Doctorate.

Pierre died tragically in a street accident in 1906. Marie was devastated. After his death the Sorbonne physics department decided to pass the chair that had been created for Pierre Curie over to Marie. She became the first woman ever to become a professor at the Sorbonne. Marie's work became widely recognised. In 1911 she was awarded her second Nobel Prize in Chemistry. It was awarded in recognition of her services to the advancement of chemistry by the discovery of the elements radium and polonium.

Marie died from aplastic anemia contracted from exposure to radiation. The damaging effects of ionizing radiation were not yet known, and a lot of her work had been carried out in a shed, without proper safety measures. Her work challenged conventional ideas in Chemistry and Physics and she also challenged gender norms by being one of the first successful female scientists.

Marie Curie
7 November 1867 –
4 July 1934

Pioneering Chemist and Physicist

Illustration by Harriet Gibson

Whose resilience inspires us?

Alison has a congenital disorder, phocomelia, which caused her to be born without arms and with truncated legs. She grew up in a children's home after a doctor recommended to her mother that, in Lapper's own words, 'it would be best if I were looked after by the state and that she should put me out of her mind.'

When she was fitted with artificial limbs, she had them only as an attempt to make her look less disconcerting, instead of actually helping her. So she abandoned them and learned to live without external aids.

At the age of 19 she moved to London. She acquired a driving licence and a flat. Lapper studied in The Faculty of Arts and Architecture at the University of Brighton and graduated with a first class honours degree in Fine Art in 1994.

Alison describes her work as follows: 'My work questions notions of physical normality and beauty, in a society that considers me to be deformed because I was born without arms. In my photographic work, I use light and shadow to create images with a sculptural quality reminiscent of classical statues.'

One particular influence is the sculpture Venus de Milo, due to the physical similarities between the idealized classical female statue and Lapper's own body.

She has taken part in various British exhibitions, including those in the Royal Festival Hall. She is a member of the Association of Mouth and Foot

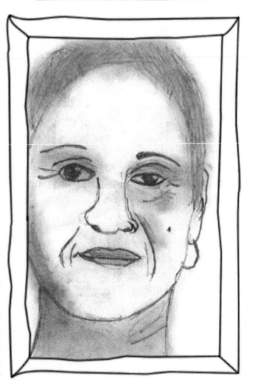

Alison Lapper
Born 7 April 1965

Fine Artist

Painting Artists of the World (Alison paints with her mouth). In May 2003, Lapper was awarded an MBE for her services to art.

Illustration by Harriet Gibson

Women supporting each other

A central part of resilience is through friendship. Having good friends, people you can trust and those who trust you is an important part of friendship. Sometimes you are the one who supports them and sometimes it's them who help you. It's more than just having a friend on a social network. These might not be real friends. They might not be people who would come round and look after you if you were poorly, or listen to you talk for an hour if you are heartbroken.

So good friends help us to be resilient. How have friends helped you to be strong?

Illustration by Omena Osivwemu

Here are some thoughts we had about friendship:

- Different levels of friendship is good, it's like a dartboard where you have just a few really good friends in the middle, and you have lots of acquaintances around the outside. We think it doesn't matter how many friends you have, it's the quality of the friends that is important
- Respect in friendship is also important. Learn each others' good and not-so-good points, but accept someone for everything that they are and try not to focus on the things that annoy you.
- Love unconditionally, don't judge just listen!
- You need friends in education, in the work place and also in your home
- Men/boyfriends/male partners. We felt that men are important to have as friends, but also that when you are growing up, sometimes it is hard to separate out friendship from someone fancying you/you fancying someone. Many people are lesbian and bisexual too, so with friends of the same sex, sometimes the lines of friendship can also be blurry. So, handle friendships with care and talk things through with people if you are not sure!
- Support is empowering - if you help someone you also learn and feel stronger. You get a gift of helping someone.
- Socialising is important, especially to meet people outside of your own age group, class, race or sexual orientation, etc. One young person talked about the importance of people with disabilities (like herself) mixing with those who do not have disabilities, as a way to both learn about each other's lives and share experiences
- Trust is important. Don't trust people too easily, get to know them first, but equally, don't be so private that people never learn about who you are. Otherwise it is hard for people to get to know you and be a true friend
- For some of us, family can be our best friends, but for others of us, we escape our family to find people who understand us. What seems to be true for many of us is that having a family, either the one we were born into or one we create from friends and lovers, is a crucial part of being able to bounce back and be resilient in life

Chapter 2 - Herstory

by Alison Ronan

Why we gathered things from under people's beds

"You can't kill the spirit, she is like the mountain, old and strong, she goes on and on."

Greenham Common chant

Panels completed by young women and youth workers across Greater Manchester and the North West, coordinated by Jenny Wynn

"When nothing is certain, everything is possible."

Vaclav Havel

n the spring 2005 I met an old youth work colleague, Jean Spence, in York Railway Station to discuss our individual research into pioneering women in early twentieth century Britain. Both of us were inspired and humbled by these feisty women. Jean was researching the girls' worker Lily Montague and I was looking at anti-war women in the First World War. These were women who were involved in early feminist work with young women, battling for the vote and involved in persistent campaigning for women's rights. We talked about the youth and community work we had been involved in since the 1970s working with girls and young women. We reflected on the battles we had been through to maintain and sustain space for girls' work. We talked and talked - about the past and the present, including the shifting political agendas in relation to feminism, the strategies of subterfuge, the friendships webs we created, and how powerful feminist youth work was. We suddenly realised that our personal and professional histories (her-stories) of feminism and feminist youth work

were in boxes under beds, on top of wardrobes, in sheds, un-catalogued and largely forgotten.

We didn't want this history, or rather herstory, to be lost. So much of women's history is forgotten, unwritten, or not prioritised by a society that values history through 'great rulers/ dictators/ tyrants' (mostly men) or through war (seen through the perspective of those fighting such wars - mostly men). For women to understand who they are, they need to know where they have come from, how women's identity and history/herstory has shaped them. We wanted to make sure that youth work with young women, and its history, was reclaimed, celebrated, and understood.

So, we decided to use our own webs, our feminist networks to get our contemporaries together to discuss a number of things:

- To reconnect with feminist youth work practice since the 70s (single sex work/arts and cultural work/ issue based work)
- To consider how feminist youth work had influenced work with girls today
- To reflect on the changing political landscape in relation to girls and young women over the last 30 years
- To create an archive of our work as a memory and as an inspiration

We decided to contact other women under the heading of **Feminist Webs.** In retrospect the use of 'webs' came with a resonance of the 1970s and 1980s, including Greenham Common Peace Camp (find out more about that in the Chapter 4). At the camp, women would hang their possessions like a big web on a huge wire fence.

The was also a chant from Greenham that went like this:

"It's not just the web it's the way we spin it, it's not just the world it's the women that's in it; that's what gets results."

Greenham Common Chant

Webs' conjures up the ideas of spinning/spinster, creativity/hope, and friendship/networking and of course the ideas of dangerous and seductive spaces. We used the word because it seemed to encapsulate the heady days of the 'telephone tree'. (Before mobiles, texts and the internet, we would create a notification diagram called a 'tree'. It would work by one person calling three people, and each one of those people calling three more, until we reached everyone who needed contacting). The web also sums up the campaigning against violence and war and the importance of women friends, colleagues and lovers that seemed to have been summed up the 70s 80s and 90s.

The Feminist Webbers later came up with this list of what the web means to them (kindly documented by Janet Bastsleer in 2010 for a book for the Open University):

- About forwardness
- About inter-connectedness
- Full of spaces
- And also lines which are the connections and the stories
- They hold people together like a net
- Points of understanding across generations
- A way of representing what feminism is and making links with other social justice movements
- Sticky - they hold people together
- Not unusual
- Not innocent - ask the fly!
- But people can get stuck in them

In the late summer of 2005, 40 women from all over the UK came together in Manchester. They were full of energy, brimming with ideas, recalling memories and eager to implement plans for the future. There was a younger energetic woman called Amelia Lee. There was a commitment to creating an archive and to using new technologies – another web, now world-wide - to publicise the work. Immediately the project became inter-generational.

We had indeed spun another Feminist Web.

Calendar made by Laurel St Young Women's Centre. The centre was originally set up in 1983 serving Norley Hall and Worsely Hall housing estates in Wigan. The calendar was donated to the Feminist Webs Archive by youth worker Marie Brookfield.

LAUREL ST.

YOUNG WOMEN'S CENTRE

1986

This is what the Feminist Webs archive means to us...

Taken from a workshop at an intergenerational event in 2009

Archive

- There for the future
- A collection of material which represents an event or subject
- Historic resources
- Never heard of it
- Past
- Store
- Collection
- Library?
- Useful resources
- Groups of memories
- YouTube
- Memories stored
- Physical library of facts

- There to achieve something
- Celebrating what has already been and planning for the future
- Book
- Record
- Open access to information
- A place where we can store objects from the past
- Emancipation, liberation, empowerment, rights.
- A collection of women's own words and stories
- Collection of resources
- Place to keep stuff in!

And this is what 'history' means to us...

- Records of past events
- Before your generation
- Boring
- 'Her'story
- Subject at school
- Old
- Stories
- School history – old stuff, old people!!!
- Movements of the past. What to do next?
- Oral history…people's stories
- Important things in the past
- Happening every second – we're creating it

- History that's not taught at school
- Is it his-story? (always about men?!)
- The importance of women's personal ideas and feelings when they are usually silenced in a male-dominated society
- Make love not war, all you hear about is war history!!!
- Good times and bad times
- Ages ago!
- Different eras or generations
- Groups of memories
- Dates and facts
- Memory narratives
- Autobiography and sometimes lies!

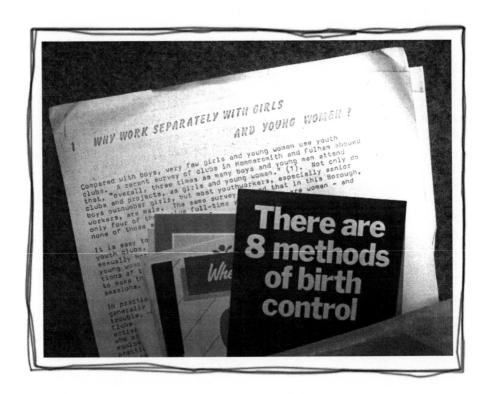

Collection of books from the Feminist Webs Archive

Our herstory of feminist youth work

In 2009 we all met together (alongside a number of young women from across the North West), and created a timeline together of feminist youth work. The timeline was done from people's memories and not intended to be exact in terms of dates, but instead was about sharing memories with each other and with younger women who knew very little about the history of feminism. We are sharing it with you here to give you some ideas of what was important to us from the 1970s onward.

Before 1970s

- 1968 Community bases and women's stuff was connected
- Fractured histories: and who passes it on, how it gets passed on
- Civil rights movement Student-led feminism, but not just middle class women - Manchester working class women, working class lesbians
- Being an 'outsider' Debates about 'which women' feminism was for
- Feminism came first – then the youth work & community work & arts practice
- The pill and debates about its real implications
- Feelings – images of protest & awareness of social justice

The 1970s

- Pubs - women knitting in male-only bars; women's groups; a half pint in a pub served in what people called 'ladies' glasses
- 1975 – Equal Pay Act. Pay in the canteen went up – by a lot!
- Abortion bills in Government
- Challenging sexism e.g. pin-ups
- Trade Union leader Arthur Scargill nude in 'Yorkshire Miner' Magazine
- Youth Clubs OK. New Forest Conference 'Girls are people too'
- Equality – women could ride motorbikes, and do DIY etc
- Big arguments between women about feminism
- 1977, Water Adventure Centre sets up first girls night in Manchester
- Home-support difficulties. How seriously are women taken
- Youth Services in Local Authorities introduce equality policies but mostly it is down to hard work of individuals rather than organisation-wide
- National and Local Girls Work Units run conferences / forums / workshops
- Miners strike
- Grassroots movements
- Women's books and publishing e.g. Virago Press
- National organisation for work with girls & young women is set up 'NOWGYW'
- Reclaim the night protests begin across the world
- 'Fight the Alton Bill' campaign so women could have reproductive rights
- Equal opportunities training & policies
- Spare Rib magazine published

The 1980s

- Women's Units in Local Authorities were set up e.g. Lancashire
- Thatcher 1979-89/Tory Government 1979-97
- Women's disability politics
- Class politics Section 28
- Support for Greenham Common
- WIGGS –Workers In Girls Groups - Coventry
- Personally, I started doing girls work (by chance) as many of us feminists did!
- Spare Rib magazine provides us with communication and inspiration
- Women's centres become more common
- HIV Education
- Youth & Community courses give us chance to study
- Black lesbian poets
- Southhall Black Sisters - Shakti
- Worked with fab women role models
- Came out
- Empowered through Clause 28 LGBT campaign, and all campaigns, in work, college
- Pride
- Lesbian strength: Zami-Audre Lorde
- Youth Clubs UK - National Youth Agency
- Magazines - resources

The 1970s

- Gillick guidelines about young people having the right to chose their own medical treatment including 'the pill'
- '90s music & KD Lang, U mag, Spice Girls - What is 'girl power'?
- Awareness & division in women's movement- things start to fragment
- Late '90s women's HIV & sexual health
- Beijing world conference on rights of women. Conjugal rights overturned
- 'Ladettes' emerged
- Janet Batsleer's book *The Bible - Working with girls & young women in community settings*
- Women's comedy - Ellen comes out as a lesbian
- Buffy and Xena on TV

2000 onwards

- 'Not For Girls' – 'Yorkie' chocolate bars adverts on TV, not as many people speak out about this as would have done in 1970s
- Rise of Paula Radcliffe, Ellen McArthur, Dame Kelly Holmes - all good sporting role models
- 'Diversity' training
- Dec '05 same-sex Civil Partnerships
- Playboy bunny pencil cases and T-shirts start to be sold to children
- '06 Section 28 repealed, allowing schools to talk about same sex relationships
- Single equality act - recognition of interconnectedness of oppression?
- Not only 'a white woman's history'

Whose resilience inspires us?

The women of our herstory are numerous. Women in your family, women who have ruled the world, supported a friend, run a country or a business or a household. Women who have cared Women who have dared.

You will find inspiring women throughout this book. We call these 'Spirit Women.' That means women whose stories and identities can guide your spirit and help you in life. On the following pages are a few more.

Whose resilience inspires us?

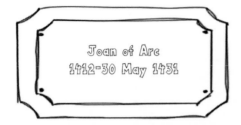

Joan of Arc
1412–30 May 1431

Saint Joan of Arc is considered a national heroine of France and a Catholic saint. She was a peasant girl born in eastern France. Joan asserted that she had visions from God that instructed her to recover her homeland from English domination.

She led the French army to several important victories during the Hundred Years' War, which paved the way for the coronation of Charles VII. She was captured by the Burgundians, sold to the English, tried by a Church court, and burned at the stake when she was 19 years old.

Twenty-five years after the execution, Pope Callixtus III examined the trial, pronounced her innocent and declared her a martyr. Joan of Arc was made a saint in 1920. She is – along with St. Denis, St. Martin of Tours, St. Louis IX, and St. Theresa of Lisieux – one of the patron saints of France.

Even today, Joan of Arc has remained a significant figure in Western culture. French politicians of all leanings have invoked her memory.

Many famous writers, film makers, video game makers, and composers have created works about her. This includes Shakespeare (Henry VI, Part 1), Verdi (Giovanna d'Arco), Tchaikovsky (The

Martyr, warrior, visionary, legend

Maid of Orleans opera), Mark Twain (Personal Recollections of Joan of Arc), Bertolt Brecht (Saint Joan of the Stockyards) and George Bernard Shaw (Saint Joan).

Illustration by Harriet Gibson

Whose resilience inspires us?

Martina Navratilova
Born 18 October 1958

Martina was born in Prague in Czechoslovakia. She started playing tennis when she young and was coached by her stepfather. In 1972 at the age of 15, Navratilova won the Czechoslovakia national tennis championship. She won her first professional singles title in Orlando, Florida. She turned professional in 1975.

At this time she asked the United States for political asylum and was granted temporary residency. Czechoslovakia responded by stripping her of citizenship. She was granted American citizenship in 1981 but in 2008 she had her Czech citizenship restored.

The greatest women's tennis player ever

In her career Martina won 18 Grand Slam singles titles, 31 Grand Slam women's doubles titles (an all-time record), and 10 Grand Slam mixed doubles titles. She reached the Wimbledon singles final 12 times, including 9 consecutive years from 1982 through 1990, and won the women's singles title at Wimbledon a record 9 times.

Off the court Martina announced that she was a lesbian in the early 1980s. At this time she had a relationship with author Rita Mae Brown, author of Rubyfruit Jungle. Martina is also involved in a lot of charity work involving underprivileged children, LGBTQI and animal rights. She is also a Health and Fitness advocate and inspires people to live healthy, active lives the world over.

Illustration by Harriet Gibson

Whose resilience inspires us?

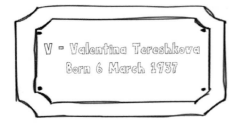

V - Valentina Tereshkova
Born 6 March 1937

Valentina was born in a village in Central Russia. Her parents had migrated from Belarus.

She became interested in parachuting from a young age, and trained in skydiving at the local Aeroclub. She made her first jump at age of 22 on 21 May 1959. At the time, she was employed as a textile worker in a local factory. It was her expertise in skydiving that led to her selection as a cosmonaut.

After the flight of Yuri Gagarin into space in 1961, there were plans to put a woman into space.

Valentina was one of the five out of more than four hundred applicants selected to join the female cosmonaut corps. She qualified because of her parachuting skill, age and weight.

In preparation of her space flight, Valentina trained hard. This included weightless flights, isolation tests, centrifuge tests, rocket theory, spacecraft engineering, 120 parachute jumps and pilot training in jet fighters. The training paid off and she was selected above the other four candidates. When she flew she was 26 years old.

During the flight she orbited the earth 48 times and spent almost three days

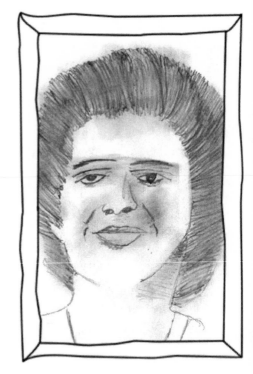

First woman in space

in space. On her return to earth she gained a doctorate in engineering. Because of her amazing achievement she then went on to pursue a successful career in politics.

Illustration by Harriet Gibson

Whose resilience inspires you?

 Create a Spirit Woman of your own - who has inspired you to be the person you are today? Write about her below.

Draw your heroine or role model in the box on the next page, or stick a photo in of her.

My spirit woman is....

Because....

The impact she has had on me is....

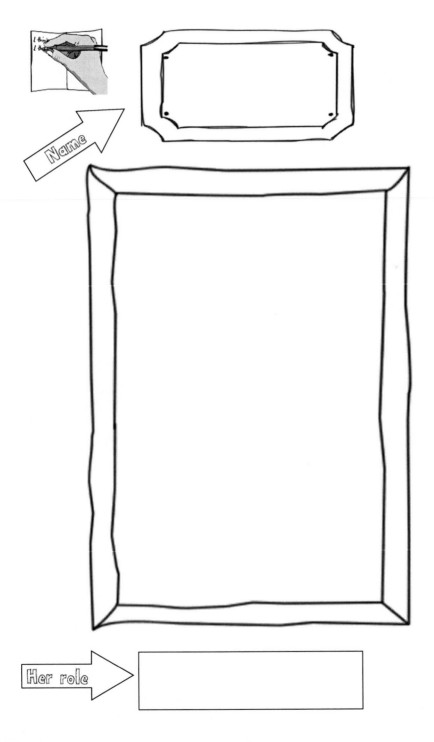

Illustration by Hebe Phillips

Where can I find out more about women's history/herstory?

Thanks to the internet and the passion and enthusiasm of lots of women, there are a number of places and organisations that you can research to find out more about women's history.

The Feminist Archive North - FAN - Leeds

The Feminist Archive North (FAN) holds a wide variety of material relating to the Women's Liberation Movement (WLM) from 1969 to the present. Topics covered by FAN include the women's peace movement, women's studies, women and development, and violence against women.

FAN was created in the 1980s, when some material from the Feminist Archive South, the sister archive founded earlier in the South-West, was relocated to the North of England. FAN was housed first in the University of Bradford and then in Leeds Metropolitan University. During this time the collection grew. In 2001 FAN was moved to Special Collections, in the Brotherton Library at the University of Leeds.

The Archive includes personal and organisational documentary archives, conference papers, dissertations, books, and complete runs of important Women's Liberation Movement magazines journals such as *Spare Rib, Shrew, Women's Report, Scarlet Woman, Shifra* and *Women's Voice*.

The Archive is regularly used by women students, academics, and activists for research and/or interest, and could be used by you if you want to have a look! If you would like more information or would like to arrange a visit with them, look them up online and contact them.

www.feministarchivenorth.org.uk

Photo taken by young Feminist Webber at a trip to the Feminist Archive North

The Women's Library - London

The Women's Library is a cultural centre housing the most extensive collection of women's history in the UK. The collections include books, pamphlets, periodicals, zines, artist books, audio-visuals, personal and organisational papers, objects, textiles and visual materials. You can visit the Reading Room to research and browse free of charge.

www.londonmet.ac.uk/thewomenslibrary

Glasgow Women's Library - Scotland

Glasgow Women's Library is a vibrant information hub housing a lending library, archive collections and contemporary and historical artefacts relating to women's lives, histories and achievements.

Glasgow Women's Library is no ordinary library! It is the only resource of its kind in Scotland and a true national treasure. The women of the library tell us why:

'As well as a lending library, we hold a wonderful treasure trove of historical and contemporary artefacts and archive materials that celebrate the lives, histories and achievements of women. From Suffragette memorabilia and 1930s dress making patterns to rare 1970s Scottish Women's Liberation newsletters, it's all here!

We also support thousands of women across Scotland every year to improve their lives through our services and programmes, including support and activities that tackle a wide range of issues from poverty and women's health, sexuality and surviving violence.

Empowering women is one of our key aims.

We have grown from a small grassroots project into the main hub for information by, for and about women in Scotland with 13 paid staff and more than 80 volunteers a year, offering specialized learning, collections and archives. GWL has always been a hotbed of ideas and is now growing into a pioneering women's social enterprise.'

www.womenslibrary.org.uk

Images from the LIK:T magazine by The Young Lesbian and Bisexual Women's Project from their trip to the Glasgow Women's Library in 2005

The Pankhurst Centre - Manchester

The birthplace of the Suffragette movement is now the Pankhurst Centre, a women's community centre in the heart of Manchester, UK. This historically tsignificant building was the home of Emmeline Pankhurst and family who led the Suffragette campaign for Votes for Women. Within the Centre there is a small heritage area with information about the Pankhursts and the Suffragette movement. This is open to the general public. As a women's community centre it provides and offers space for activities and events run by women for women. It offers a unique place in which women can learn together, work on projects and socialise. This vibrant centre plays host to a number of women's organisations and projects that support women.

www.thepankhurstcentre.org.uk

The Feminist Library - London

The Feminist Library is a large archive collection of Women's Liberation Movement literature, particularly second-wave materials dating from the late 1960s to the 1990s. We support researchers, activists and community projects in this field.

www.feministlibrary.co.uk

How to gather herstory

Everyday histories of women's lives are not often thought of as important so lots of history books don't include them! But we think they are very important!

If you like the idea of collecting history, or herstory, you can do it yourself!

In the past many women could not read or write and were not taught these skills, because educating women was not seen as important or 'ladylike'. Even today, in lots of parts of the world, some people prioritise educating their male children instead of girls. This means that a lot of women never write down their experiences or the experiences of women they know.

For this reason we encourage you to collect 'oral history' as well as things that have been written down.

We have frequently never been able to retrace the lives of poorer women, black women, lesbians or other women who have not been privileged, because we have not had a written record of what they have done. Some women such as the former slave (and amazing feminist) Sojourner Truth, had another woman write their story down for them. Even through Sojourner was a great public speaker, she could not read and write.

Oral history is really important...
This is what oral history means to us:

- The spoken word
- Talking to each other, exchange
- Word of mouth
- Verbalising feelings, frustrations, happiness, etc
- Discussion and expression
- Talking out loud, your life is important enough to be heard
- Opinions
- Chat
- Telling people about you

So, if you want to make sure the stories and lives of women are recorded for future generations (remember that this is making history/herstory for the future), then get a paper and pen, a camera, voice recorder/ dicta-phone or a film camera and start recording, writing, clicking...!

You can do this for fun, just have lots of conversations with people, or you might want to make it more of a project. If it's going to be a project, on the next page there are some tips from us...

- Write down lots of questions to ask people
- Ask them to give you written permission to record them
- Get them to think about the questions before you meet with them e.g. send them the questions in advance or encourage them to dig out old photos or booklets to help trigger their memories
- Keep their contact details so you can get in touch if you forgot to ask the something
- Use the recordings e.g. have a display at a local school or library, or send them to you nearest sound archive so they can keep them safe for the future

Here is some space to write down some things you find out about the herstories of older women you know, facts, stories, old loves, great and not so great things about what is was like for them growing up as a girl etc etc etc:

 Herstory....

Herstory....

Chapter 3 - Banged up and banged up

This chapter is about prison, and about pregnancy. The two sit together here because it made a catchy chapter heading, and not because we think pregnancy is like a prison! To pretend that pregnancy and maternity is always good for women though, would be to make a great mistake. Feminism is about choices, the choice to have, or not to have children; to decide on the method of birth (if you do have children); and to decide how much our bodies are 'medicalised'. But enough about pregnancy... let's start with being banged up in the prison-sense and see where that takes us...

Banged up

by Joan Meredith

In 1997 Sir David Ramsbotham, Chief Inspector of Prisons, made an unannounced inspection of Holloway women's prison. Conditions there were so appalling that he suspended the inspection and walked out.

The Government has never given priority to the treatment of the disadvantaged, 'invisible' women in society. Prison is used as a convenient tool of social control. Half of women prisoners have dependent children; a quarter of all women prisoners have been in care; half have suffered domestic violence; their mental and physical health is poor and 60% are drug or alcohol dependent. How shocking that death due to neglect and suicide and self-harm are routine in women's prisons?

In 1993 the number of women detained in prison was 560, about 1 per cent of the prison population. There was a steep rise in sentencing for men and women from 1993-2003 (statistics.gov.uk). In 2003 there were 4461 women in prison and around this time the highest number of recorded suicides took place.

Various people and groups have raised concerns over this issue. These include the Fawcett Society, Debbie Coles of INQUEST (co-author of *Dying on the Inside*), individuals like prison inspectors and experts like Professor David Wilson (author of *Death at the Hands of the State*).

It appears that all of these objections are simply ignored by those in power.

The Corston Report 2007 called for a radical overhaul of the treatment of women in jail. It argued that prisons should be abolished because the conditions are so bad.

Pauline Campbell was a prison reform activist. Her daughter Sarah Campbell died in Styal Prison (Cheshire, England) in the so-called 'care' of the state. Pauline ran her own campaign, to shame the Home Office and shake its indifference about the poor treatment of women in prison. She was arrested more than a dozen times for protesting outside prisons, and at aged 60, Pauline herself died, her body found by the gravestone of her daughter.

In 2005 Anne Owers, Chief Prison Inspector, reported that Holloway remained an extremely difficult prison to run. It was cleaner, but there were still problems. Like all other women's prisons, she said, it was holding women who should 'not be there and whose continued imprisonment was would do more harm to their lives, the prisons and the long term interests of society at large.' (news.bbc.co.uk)

With the number of women in prison predicted to rise in the coming years (and a male-dominated Criminal Justice System), things look as though they could worse. Thankfully we have some good campaigning groups such as 'Women in Prison' (womeninprison.org.uk) who are striving to raise awareness of the bad treatment many women face, and to improve things for women prisoners.

Whose resilience inspires us?

Elizabeth Fry
21 May 1780 -
12 October 1845

Elizabeth was born in Norwich into a Quaker family. Her Mother died when she was twelve and Elizabeth was partly responsible for the care and training of the younger children. Elizabeth had eleven children of her own.

Following her marriage to Joseph Fry in 1800, the couple moved to the outskirts of London. Upon recommendation from a friend she visited Newgate prison. Elizabeth was appalled at what she saw. The women's section was overcrowded with women and children, some of whom had not even received a trial. Elizabeth sometimes stayed overnight in prisons, and invited nobility to come and stay so they could see what it was like. She made friends with many of the women prisoners because of this.

In 1817 she helped found the Association for the Reformation of the Female Prisoners in Newgate. This led to the eventual creation of the British Ladies' Society for Promoting the Reformation of Female Prisoners. This organization is widely thought to be the first nationwide women's organization in Britain. Elizabeth was a major driving force behind new legislation to make the treatment of prisoners more humane, and she was supported in her efforts by the reigning monarch.

Prison reformer, Quaker and Philanthropist

She is also the first woman to present evidence in Parliament.

Illustration by Harriet Gibson

Women in prison - Why the numbers don't add up to make justice

by Viv Whittaker

Prison is often a very expensive way of making vulnerable women's life situations much worse. Many believe that prison does not work and agree that the best way to cut women's offending is to deal with its root causes.

One woman who believed this and whom herself had served "time" in Holloway prison, vowed that on her release she would do whatever it would take to support women (both inside and outside). She wanted to support not punish women.

Her name was Chris Tchaikovsky, who sadly died in 2002, aged 57.

Chris, a former founder of the charity 'Women in Prison', believed that:

*"***Taking** the most hurt people out of society and punishing them in order to teach them how to live within society is, at best, futile. Whatever else a prisoner knows, she knows everything there is to know about punishment because that is exactly what she has grown up with. Whether it is childhood sexual abuse, indifference, neglect; punishment is most familiar to her.*"*

www.womeninprison.org.uk

Prison causes damage and disruption to the lives of vulnerable women, most of whom pose no risk to the public. Women have been and are marginalised within the criminal justice system. For example, if a woman has stolen food to feed her children or not paid her TV licence, and breaches her bail because her child is sick, she can end up in prison. And what then happens to her children? They often end up being taken into care, which punishes a whole family. The woman herself is no danger to society but is put in prison regardless. Women prisoners are much more likely to be solely responsible for the care of children and the maintenance of a home than male prisoners. Because of this, prison impacts disproportionately harshly on many women prisoners, often resulting in the loss of a home and serious disruption to the lives of their children.

There are only 14 female prisons in England and none in Wales – so often women get incarcerated miles from their homes and families, this makes visits very difficult for a woman's children and family.

Women in prison often lose their homes, their relationships with their children, and their mental health in the process. All of this when the majority of sentenced female prisoners are held for non-violent offences!

I have worked with women who come out of prison after a 6 month sentence for 'repeated shoplifting', and they have lost their homes, their child or children have gone into care, and they end up living in a homeless hostel.

To re-build your life after this experience is quite a challenge, and many agencies and support services are much needed at this time in a woman's life and should be readily available. The cost to keep a woman in prison for 12 months is approx £56,000 – or a community service with support would cost approx £10,000 - £15,000 – I know which option I think is best!

- In the years building up to 1918, did you know that many women went to prison when they were campaigning for the right to vote? Many would go on hunger-strike and classed themselves as political prisoners. When they were too sick from starvation, they would be released, so that the state could not say they were responsible for their death. Some women who did get better would dress in disguise and be smuggled away so they could not be re-arrested

- Did you know that many women were arrested and sent to prison for creating a huge permanent camp at Greenham Common, England, to protest about Nuclear disarmament? (Cruise Missiles were going to be stored at the American airbase there)

- Women peace activists have been arrested all over the world for standing up for their rights

Whose resilience inspires us?

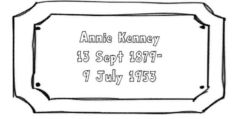

Annie Kenney
13 Sept 1879–
9 July 1953

Annie Kenney was born at Springhead into a working class family. Annie's mother and father worked in the Oldham textile industry. When Annie was 10 she went to work in a local cotton mill. The working conditions were poor and a whirling bobbin tore off her finger! By the age of 13 she worked full-time in the mill. She also worked hard at home, helping with cooking and cleaning.

Although Annie had no formal education, her mother encouraged her to read. She read many of the free thinkers of the time, such as Edward Carpenter and Walt Whitman. Annie was inspired by her readings and joined the Independent Labour Party.

Militant Suffragette

In 1905 Annie saw Christabel Pankhurst speak about Women's Right to get the Vote. She was so impressed with what she heard she decided to join the Women's Social and Political Union, the militant branch of the suffragettes. She soon moved to London to help with the cause. Annie became trusted with important organisational roles for the WSPU and worked in London, Bristol, America and Australia.

Annie was imprisoned on several occasions for her 'militant' activism, which included disrupting political meetings and setting fire to post boxes. Like many other suffragettes, she partook in hunger strikes. She stood by her militancy, seeing it as a key part in the successful struggle for women's suffrage.

Illustration by Harriet Gibson

Criminal Justice in summary

The reality today is that prisons are dangerous, especially for women. David Wilson in his book *Death At The Hands Of The State* published by The Howard League believes that we must go beyond reform and abolish prisons altogether. Pauline Campbell whose daughter died in prison 2003 took direct action stopping prison vans from entering the prison every time a woman died. She campaigned to raise awareness of how awful and barbaric this side of British public life really is. Vulnerable women need help. Locking them up in overcrowded prisons solves nothing. There is a lot of evidence to say that things need to change. Women need to support these campaigns.

What can you do?

Write a letter or poem to your MP and tell them that they need to do something!

Write a letter to a woman in your local prison, tell them about your life and ask them to tell you about their life. This will help them feel human again.

Women, sex and pregnancy
How much do you know about your bits?

by Ali Hanbury

Have a look at this picture and see which bits you can name. Answers are at the end of the chapter!

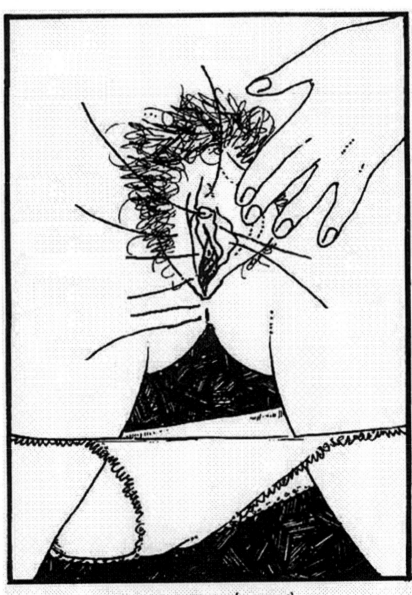

female anatomy (external)

Often, when we are asked 'what's the difference between men and women?' one of the answers is 'women get pregnant.' This is true, but they can't do it alone. If a child asks 'where do babies come from?' What would you say in response?

Here a few answers: Men and women have sex, a man and a woman love each other and have a special 'hug', a doctor helps put the baby in the belly, a stalk delivers it, it happens as a result of rape, a sperm/egg donor helps out, they are adopted...the list of possibilities is too long to write here!

Throughout history, our thoughts on being a woman, having sex and getting pregnant has been viewed in very different ways.

- The Contraceptive Pill wasn't available to women until 1961 in the U.K

- In the 1600s women were sometimes married off aged as young as 12, and began to have children in their early teens (13/14 years old!).This was considered normal and expected

- Women would be expected to "let" their husbands have sex with them, even if the woman didn't want sex. This is known as Marital Rape, and was not made illegal in the UK until 1991

- In the 1950s, '60s and '70s sex was seen as something primarily for men, and it was considered embarrassing for women to talk about (or have) orgasms. Some women set up 'consciousness raising' groups. These were groups where women got together to talk about issues, inequality they faced, through this also got to know themselves better. Some of these groups included women finding out about, and looking at their clitoris, with an emphasis on the fact that IT IS OK FOR WOMEN TO KNOW ABOUT THEIR BODIES AND GET PLEASURE FROM SEX

Design-a-vagina

As part of a project to 'get to know your bits,' some young women created pretend vaginas, gave them a name, worked out how they would talk, what clothes they might wear etc etc! Why not create your own design-a-vagina here:

Name:

Voice:

Where she likes to socialise:

Hobbies:

What clothes she likes to wear:

What she thinks about herself:

Draw your Design-a-vagina here:

Thankfully many things have improved since women started to reclaim their sexuality in the 1970s, but other things haven't changed as much as we'd like:

- There is no requirement for schools to teach sex and relationship education
- Sexualisation of young girls is on the increase in the media such as girls magazines, Playboy Bunny pencil cases, the 'acceptance' of pole dancing, high heels for babies, and computer games glamorising violence towards woman such as Grand Theft Auto
- The rise of 'sexting' (where boys circulate via text message topless or naked pictures of girls they know)

- Some people argue that the contraceptive pill was not tested enough before it was launched. Now that millions of women use it, we do not necessarily know if this will result in long term health problems for women or any children they have
- In Germany where prostitution is legalised, unemployed women are being offered jobs by the job centre in Brothels. One woman who refused to take the job now risks having her benefits cut! (www.telegraph.co.uk)

These are thoughts by Feminist Webber Kimberley Osivwemu during the Body Image project:

How is woman composed - not just a breast, a boob, an expression of mammary gland. Not just a grope, a prod, a casual cursory look! A woman is more than a series of shapes stuck together in tessellation.

Kimerley Osiuwemu - Feminist Webs - 14.3.09

Here are some key sex, pregnancy and relationships questions to consider...

- Who do you have sex with and why?
- Is sex pleasurable for you?
- What actually is sex?
- Do you want to be a parent some day?
- How will you become pregnant if you do, or avoid it if you don't?

- Are women treated differently to men?
- What does it mean to be a 'woman'?
- If you are a lesbian, is pregnancy part of your world/ your future or not? (remember either of these are fine!)

These are difficult questions to answer, and they may change throughout your life.

Sexuality Flower

This Sexuality Flower drawing shows how many different aspects - or 'petals' - there are that make up our sexuality. Some people think - and the media, advertising, music videos and so on reinforce this - that our sexuality is all about sex. It's not - it's much wider and more about our whole selves and our whole lives than that. You don't have to have sex to have a sexuality - this Flower shows some of the many ways in which we can feel and express our sexuality.

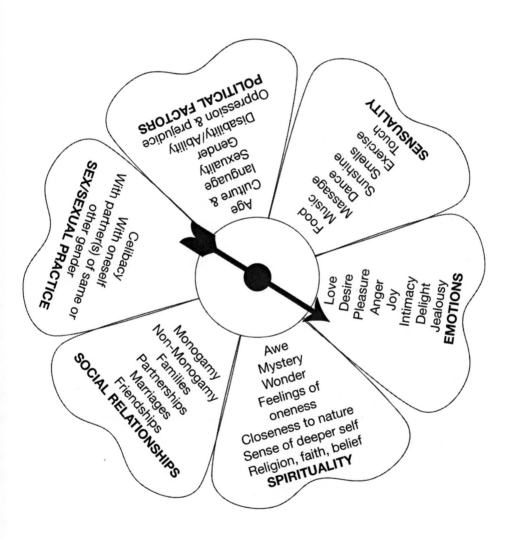

Created by Jo Adams
www.sexualhealthsheffield.nhs.uk/wp-content/uploads/2011/05/Explore-Dream-Discover.pdf

During sex and relationships...

Just remember, you have the right to be safe from harm and also not to harm others. You have the right to be respected and to respect those around you. You have the right to consent to relationships and sex and must also check that others consent to them too.

 Consent - Verb

1. To give your agreement

2. To permit something to take place after considering your options

Smears and Injections - what is it all about?

Hi, my name is Razia. I volunteer for Brook Sexual Health Charity. In my role as part of Brook Manchester's Education Team, I have learnt a lot about topics relating to sexual health. Before this, I was both oblivious to, (and sometimes felt uncomfortable talking about) things to do with sex. I also found it difficult to truly express my thoughts. After coming to Brook, I started to feel more confident in conversing with others about sexual health.

The one project I enjoyed the most was during cervical cancer awareness week and testicular cancer awareness month in June. We participated in sessions with a community artist, and produced ducks and penguins with speculums for beaks. (Which you can see over the page). We also transformed speculums into flower pots. This was to try and reduce anxiety about cervical screening, also known as a smear test. Lots of girls are worried about having a smear test but it is ok when you have one. They can help Doctors check that everything is ok with your cervix and vaginal area. We also talked about the HPV vaccine which can help stop some cervical cancers, but some people are not sure of it as it does seem to have some negative side effects.

Being with the group of volunteers made it really fun and interesting, and helped us learn about these issues. It was a very successful project. We used the ducks as a display in the clinical waiting area. I learnt a lot and enjoyed it very much. I have since been involved in creating lots of ideas for our event for sexual health awareness week in September and for how we can be more involved in the Sex:Positive campaign.

Made by Brook Manchester Young Volunteers

Feminist Webs as a learning opportunity - thinking about pregnancy

By Kimberley Osivwemu 17.5.09

A **portmanteau word** is a word that blends two or more words together e.g. smoke and fog blended makes 'smog' or Brad and Angelina make 'Brangelina'.

Pregdote - is a **portmanteau word**. It comes from blending the word 'pregnancy' with the word 'anecdote' (a little snapshot/short story)

Pregdote means...

My practice as a youth worker certainly predates the birth of most of the young women in the Feminist Webs Project. I am proud to say many young people I have worked with are now parents. I regularly revisit, unlearn and relearn as part of my practice as a youth and community worker. So here goes, I'm hoping you learn from this reflective journey.

In this piece I present the idea **pregdote** as a result of studying current media. During one Feminist Webs workshop we were introduced to the way that women are dissected for consumption and commodified into different body parts. The popular media does this a lot. This results in a focus on what the body looks like rather than what it can do. Heterosexuality is promoted as healthy through this 'dissection' of the female body. This is even more pronounced through the dissection of the female pregnant body. This focuses on what the body looks like rather than what it can do.

The 'pregdote' is used by the

A POEM - or CHANT

Bottoms, boobs and body bits!
Is that all that woman is?
A tousled hair, a flash of tit.
Bottoms boobs and body bits!

Bottoms, boobs and body bits!
Is that all that woman is?
An altered boob a nipped in tuck.
Is that all that woman is?

Bottoms, boobs and body bits!
Is that all that woman is?
A fertile tube, a rounded hip.

---

contemporary media e.g. magazines, to communicate anecdotal stories of celebrity pregnancy and motherhood. Through the pregdote we consume women as pregnant items of consumption. We scrutinise their pre-birth regimes, weight, medication, and dietary supplements There is a culture of confessional pregnancy stories. Pregnant female bodies have become object of the mass media. Women are judged and scrutinised at a point in their lives when they might just want to enjoy being pregnant without the pressure of how they look/what they weigh.

How valuable is pregnancy and mothers in our society?

My observation is we have made some progress for pregnancy and motherhood to get the status they both deserve, but very little.

Angela Davis drew distinctions around African American choices about pregnancy and childbirth when she looked at the assumptions made in campaigns to position choices with women. She drew on the experience of oppressed women choosing to self-abort, graphically described by Toni Morrison in *Beloved*.

Our society tells us that girls and women have control and choice. A common assumption is that pregnancy is chosen and that women have mastered contraception, health and methods of birthing. It is assumed that we are now able, willing and expected to control when we have children, if at all.

There is an illusion that all women and girls are equal in their birthing choices. But this is not the case.

There are disparities still in the prenatal health and postnatal survival of black and minority ethnic girls and women in the UK. I wonder why this is? Are there still disparities of value placed on girls and women's contributions to society? It seems to me that the meter is still the same. My childbearing capacity is not valued: Is not seen as an important role.

The potential of my labours as a mother is not valued. The voluntary nature of childbearing and birthing has been touched on in the cases involving surrogacy where women have claimed expenses for carrying, nurturing and delivering a live birth child. There have been attempts at costing how much a male partner should insure himself for the cost of his female partner's domestic work, and countless baby cost calculators predict the amounts of money needed to raise a child: Yet a financial approach has not promoted the true value that birth mothers contribute.

This first point relates to the way we value work. In our capitalist society valued work is rewarded with money. I am reminded of campaigns such as Wages for Housework, and wonder how far we have progressed in the endeavour for recognition of the contribution made by women in gendered roles.

Ann Oakley's *Sex, Gender and Society* (1972) argued that so-called female tasks such as mothering and housework were given lower status than so-called male tasks, therefore giving women a lower status in society. How far have we moved on from this position?

We currently have a logjam of well-founded equal pay claims that have not been settled. Some of these have been met with stone walling (silence) from local authorities, who have given women lower wage packets because they are, (or potentially could be), mothers. How can we argue that progress has been made in the recognition of women as workers regardless of their capacity to mother?

Oakley's prediction of 1972 was not far short of our current position when she said 'the differentiation of work-roles by gender will persist, and secondly, the belief that there are innate sex differences in temperament will appear to be vindicated.' (Oakley 1972 206)

Indeed it could be considered that the status 'mother' detracts from the status 'worker' leaving women with contradictory positions.

Let's reclaim early theory that motherhood and mothering does not limit our personal capacity to earn, develop careers or work.

At present much debate has been had about 'Carer's leave', 'Maternity leave', post and pre-maternal health. But how far have we come? these questions will guide us in the next stage of Feminist Webs.

Abortion

By Amelia Lee

Many feminists, but not all, are in favour or a woman's 'right to choose.' This means to choose if, whether and how women have children. For many people, the 'right to choose' includes the right to have an abortion. Here is a summary of where lots of feminists sit on this issue:

In favour of Abortion rights because...

- Often women in the past who had 'back street' (illegal) abortions did it because they were poverty and/ or in a desperate situation. So if it is made illegal people will still have abortions but these will be more risky because they have to do them 'undercover'
- Every 8 minutes a woman dies in the world as the result of an unsafe illegal abortion
- In 1803 you could be put to death for having an abortion (through a law called the Ellenborough Act), and in 1861 you could be looking at life imprisonment
- From 1923-1933, Fifteen per cent of maternal deaths were due to abortion e.g. *"In the thirties, my aunt died self-aborting. She had three children and couldn't feed a fourth ... So she used a knitting needle. She died of septicaemia leaving her children motherless."* www.abortionrights.org.uk
- In 1967 abortion was made legal under certain circumstances. Anti-abortion groups have challenged it ever since

Against Abortion rights because...

- Some women get pressured into having an abortion by their boyfriends or family, when they would like to have the baby. They feel that they would be unsupported if they went through with the pregnancy so are forced to have a termination
- In some parts of the world women have also been forced into being sterilised
- If women always felt able to use contraception, were educated in how to use it properly and always had consensual sex, would there be as much demand for abortion?
- Some women struggle with the mental impact of an abortion and carry round guilt or grief with them for the rest of their lives
- We don't know enough about embryos and foetuses to really know when life starts, including at what stage they begin to feel pain. Is it inhumane to terminate a life of a foetus that might already feel pain?

Wendy Savage and how women's bodies belong to them...

You would think that women would be ideal for jobs specialising in childbirth and pregnancy because, well, they know a little bit about what giving birth is all about, as many of us have had children/helped our pregnant friends or family members.

But the medical profession in 1969 seemed to disagree. When Wendy Savage, (who happened to be a mother of four young children), wanted to enter the medical field, her senior consultant said 'there's no place in gynaecology and obstetrics for women.'

Wendy Savage was an obstetrician and gynaecologist at the Royal London Hospital, when she was suspended for 'incompetence'.

Was she incompetent? No, was the resounding answer from the enquiry, but the medical profession appeared to be. She wrote a book called *A Savage Enquiry* (1986) where she challenged the fact that Consultants played such a big role in women giving birth. She

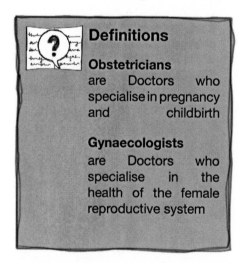

Definitions

Obstetricians are Doctors who specialise in pregnancy and childbirth

Gynaecologists are Doctors who specialise in the health of the female reproductive system

argued they were too quick to move to surgery for women who may not have needed it. (e.g. caesareans, the operation where women's abdomen's are cut through to take out the baby)

She wrote:

'Obstetricians justify their takeover of birth by reference to the improved outlook for mother and baby, and although there have been many advances for which women are grateful, there are still a large number of situations about which doctors lack adequate information to say which is the best course of action. My philosophy, in which I am not alone, of involving the woman in the decisions about her care, means that the obstetrician must relinquish some power.' (pp. 176 - Savage Enquiry 1986)

What Wendy and a number of other feminists in this field point to is that:

- Doctors need to work in partnership with women to work out the best care for pregnant women
- It is bizarre and wrong that this field of medicine was out of bounds to women for so long, when some of us are clearly very good at it, given that many women have had first hand experience of birth
- Women's bodies are their bodies. They can choose to take things to relieve pain, to have an operation or not, to give birth in a pool listening to whale music and eating prunes if they really want... AS LONG AS THE ARE ARMED WITH INFORMATION TO BE ABLE TO MAKE THESE CHOICES AND ARE EMPOWERED BY THEIR DOCTORS AND MIDWIVES

Answers - How much do you know about your bits?

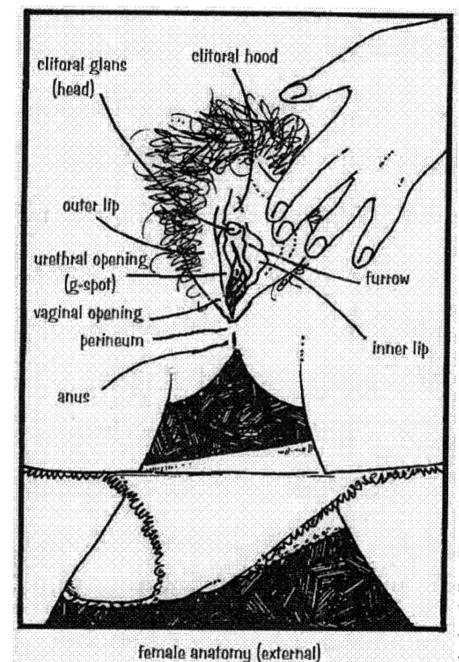

clitoral glans (head)

clitoral hood

outer lip

urethral opening (g-spot)

vaginal opening

perineum

anus

furrow

inner lip

female anatomy (external)

Chapter 4 - Riot...

By Alison Ronan

Borrowing an idea from Sue O'Sullivan

"Riot don't diet" - standing up for freedom, dreamers and dissenters or "I used to be nice"

'Go on', said Amelia, 'write something about why women need to be naughty'.

Aren't words remarkable?

To be 'naughty'.

Are we as feminists 'naughty'?

Is feminism about subverting the accepted order? Of course girls may still be described as 'Sugar and spice and all things nice,' but what about the girl who doesn't *want* to be nice? And if we, as women, are being called naughty, does it imply that women are like children, disobedient and in need of being kept in our place?

Naughty - *Adj*

1. To subvert the expected order of things, to be mischievous, or to be bad, improper or disobedient. Often used with regard to children

of feminism? Perhaps the exciting life of being a woman is also about knowing when to break the rules, to be 'naughty'?

But life as a woman who breaks the rules can be dangerous. Women who step across a line drawn in the sand by their communities and their culture can be isolated, imprisoned or even killed. So we must be careful, we must learn strategies of 'subterfuge' (to conceal, escape, and deceive). We go undercover. We create networks of support (if we are lucky). We recognise our own strengths. If we are not 'naughty', then we are moulded by society. We have to fit with what other people expect from us. So if we want to be truly free, we must accept that sometimes we need to break the rules.

and what are you going to be when you grow up, little girl?

HORRIBLE

Illustration by Jackie Fleming

Do women need to break the 'rules' in order to highlight the global threats to hard earned women's rights? How far is a woman's personal life, naughty or otherwise, also the political reality

Greenham Common Newsletter donated to Feminist Webs Archive

So when I think about what being 'naughty' might have meant to us older feminists, a few words and phrases came into my mind:

Spare Rib

Feminist magazine of the '70-90s. (So called because of the Biblical story that stated that the first woman - Eve - was created from the spare rib of a man)

Riot don't diet

- Who decides how I should look, and how do I challenge this?

Reclaim the night marches

- I want to walk about safely and will march for my right to do so

You can't kill the spirit -

- I'll never give up! Became a famous slogan

A front cover design from the infamous feminist magazine Spare Rib, which ran from the early 1970s to early 1990s

Trouble and strife

- Feminist magazine '80s-90s (That posed the question Who says I am difficult?)

Shocking Pink

- Young women's magazine '80s (I dress like a girl but – beware!)

There is no doubt that society is fascinated by women who transgress. Women who stand up to be counted and are regarded as 'naughty.'

I want to look at these women in another light – not as *naughty* but as standing up for their *human rights as women*.

Do you know about these women?

- The suffragettes who chained themselves to railings, refused food in prison and were prepared to be force-fed in their campaign for the vote
- The Chilean women who demanded to know what had happened to the disappeared activists (the *desaparecidos)* under the dictatorship of General Pinochet in the 1970s and 1980s
- The Asian women strikers at the Grunwick plant asking for equal pay and work conditions (1976-78)
- The women marching against violence in the Reclaim the Night marches
- The women campaigning against nuclear warfare at Greenham Common
- The bravery of civil rights campaigner Rosa Parks who refused, as a black woman, to be forced to sit at the back of the bus, separate to white people who were allowed to sit at the front

- The audacity of the women who had mass 'sleepovers' at their houses in 1911, to distort the Census data. They said, 'we don't have the vote, so you say we don't count. Therefore, don't count us!'
- The determined heroism of Burma's human rights activist Aung San Suu Kyi, who won the Nobel Peace prize in 1991, and spent 15 of the past 21 years under house arrest, after winning an election and opposing a military dictatorship
- These women, these acts of bravery, remind women everywhere of the fragility of women's rights and the vulnerability of global human rights. In the words of bell hooks (in *Teaching to Transgress* 1994), we must 'teach ourselves to transgress' in order to keep women's rights and human rights on the political map

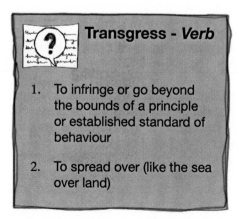

Transgress - *Verb*

1. To infringe or go beyond the bounds of a principle or established standard of behaviour

2. To spread over (like the sea over land)

Illustration by Jackie Fleming

To riot rather than diet may be fun, it may create a sense of sisterhood, it may remind us of Jackie Fleming's cartoon 'Never give up!' Naughty may even be nice or perhaps even fun! For example, lots of young women joined in the 'find out about the history of women pirates' workshop at the latest Feminist Webs event, the Carnival of Resilience.

But, it is important to remember that to be 'naughty' or disruptive can be a feminist and a political issue. Sometimes we all need to be disruptive to help ourselves, and the world around us! But the success of this relies on us, although all very different women, uniting together, agreeing what we can can collectively 'riot' for and reflecting on how we do it.

Riot Grrrl Movement

The Riot Grrrl Movement began in the early 1990s by Washington State band Bikini Kill and lead singer Kathleen Hanna, who set about making women's music super cool and super empowering.

The riot grrrl manifesto was published 1991 in the *BIKINI KILL ZINE 2,* reprinted here because we think it rocks, thank you Kathleen Hanna...

RIOT GRRRL MANIFESTO

BECAUSE us girls crave records and books and fanzines that speak to US that WE feel included in and can understand in our own ways.

BECAUSE we wanna make it easier for girls to see/hear each other›s work so that we can share strategies and criticize-applaud each other.

BECAUSE we must take over the means of production in order to create our own meanings

BECAUSE viewing our work as being connected to our girlfriends-politics-real lives is essential if we are gonna figure out how what we are doing impacts, reflects, perpetuates, or DISRUPTS the status quo.

BECAUSE we recognize fantasies of Instant Macho Gun Revolution as impractical lies meant to keep us simply dreaming instead of becoming our dreams AND THUS seek to create revolution in our own lives every single day by envisioning and creating alternatives to the bullshit christian capitalist way of doing things.

BECAUSE we want and need to encourage and be encouraged in the face of all our own insecurities, in the face of beergutboyrock that tells us we can't play our instruments, in the face of 'authorities' who say our bands/zines/etc are the worst in the US BECAUSE we don't wanna assimilate to someone else's (boy) standards of what is or isn't.

RIOT GRRRL MANIFESTO continued...

BECAUSE we are unwilling to falter under claims that we are reactionary 'reverse sexists' AND NOT THE TRUEPUNKROCKSOULCRUSADERS THAT WE KNOW we really are.

BECAUSE we know that life is much more than physical survival and are patently aware that the punk rock 'you can do anything' idea is crucial to the coming angry grrrl rock revolution which seeks to save the psychic and cultural lives of girls and women everywhere, according to their own terms, not ours.

BECAUSE we are interested in creating non-heirarchical ways of being AND making music, friends, and scenes based on communication & understanding, instead of competition & good/bad categorizations.

BECAUSE doing/reading/seeing/hearing cool things that validate and challenge us can help us gain the strength and sense of community that we need in order to figure out how bullshit like racism, able-bodieism, ageism, speciesism, classism, thinism, sexism, anti-Semitism and heterosexism figures in our own lives.

BECAUSE we are angry at a society that tells us Girl = Dumb, Girl = Bad, Girl = Weak.

BECAUSE we are unwilling to let our real and valid anger be diffused and/or turned against us via the internalization of sexism as witnessed in girl/girl jealousism and self defeating girltype behaviors.

BECAUSE I believe with my wholeheartmindbody that girls constitute a revolutionary soul force that can, and will change the world for real.

Sofia Antonia Milone, GeEkgiRL
Manchester UK based band
Photo by Tamzin Forster

Whose resilience inspires us?

Angela Y Davis
Born 26 January 1944

Davis was born in Birmingham, Alabama, USA. She grew up in a neighbourhood marked by racial conflict.

While at school she applied to study in New York at a school for Black and White people. In the South of America where she lived, Black and White people were forced to go to separate schools. She was accepted into the mixed school in New York, and it was here she became influenced by Communist ideas.

In the 1960s Davis studied French and Philosophy at University in the USA and Europe. She often aroused suspicion from US Intelligence forces (FBI) because of her involvement with Communist politics. By 1969 she was working as an Assistant Professor at UCLA and was renowned as a feminist, communist and member of the Black Panther Party, an organisation fighting for the liberation of Black people.

In 1970 Davis became an accessory to a political murder that had taken place in the name of the Black Panther Party. The FBI issued a warrant for her arrest and she fled California. Eventually she was found and arrested. A massive nationwide campaign followed calling for her release. Thanks in part to this, she was freed in 1972 after spending nearly 2 years in jail.

Writer and Social Justice Activist

Her experience in prison led to her becoming a major activist voice in the prison abolition movement in the USA.

Throughout her life Angela Davis has criticised sexism, racism, imperialism and prisons while speaking out in support of gay, lesbian, bisexual and transgender rights. She has written numerous books on these subjects and continues to be active today. She is a black lesbian and a role model for everyone.

Illustration by Harriet Gibson

Angela Davies made out of bottle tops made by Lesbian and Gay Youth Manchester

If you have been reading this book from the start, you will have already come across **Greenham Common** and you might be thinking 'Well what's all that about then?' We thought it's high time we explained it in a bit more detail, and what better place than in the 'Riot' section!

The Greenham Common Women's Peace Camp

by Margaret
Beetham and
Janet Batsleer

Photo from Greenham Common showing the fence around the military base

carrying missiles getting out), cut the perimeter fence and did other creative stunts that drew attention to the threat of nuclear war.

In December 1982, 30,000 women came from all over the country and beyond, to join hands around the 9 miles of perimeter fencing to 'Embrace the base.' In the days before email and photocopiers, this was organized by groups contacting each other, setting up telephone-trees, producing mimeographed sheets (like a photocopy but made by having to turn a crank on a machine rather than by electricity!) and doing training in non-violent resistance within local activist groups.

The Greenham Common Women's Peace Camp grew out of a 1981 march led by a group of women. They walked from Cardiff to Greenham in Berkshire to protest the American nuclear-tipped Cruise missiles that were stored there. Ignored by the base commander, the protesters set up a peace camp outside the gate. It became women-only the following year. From that grew a series of camps around the base. Amazingly the protest lasted nineteen years.

Over those years tens of thousands of women came to the camp, some just for a day, some for a short visit, some for years. They lived in harsh conditions, in home made tents called 'benders' that were made from sticks with cloth spread over them. These women were harassed by bailiffs sent to evict them, by the police, the military and by vigilante groups. They were committed to non-violent resistance actions. They blocked the gates (to stop lorries

Image taken by Feminist Webs at a Reclaim the Night March around 2008/9

Greenham was organised in a non-hierarchical way, which means there was no 'boss' and instead everyone had a say in decisions, (this was sometimes quite a difficult way of working but one that encouraged creativity). The wire fence around the base was constantly being cut, but it also became a changing art gallery that women decorated with pictures, small domestic objects, and letters. A repertoire of Greenham songs was developed and circulated on mimeographed sheets. One night a group of women entered the base and danced on the silos where the missiles were stored.

The peace camp became a national and international beacon of a new kind of politics. It was the place where a generation of women learnt about political organizing. Eventually the Government signed the treaty agreeing to remove the missiles and the American troops left in 1992. In 2000 the land was restored to the people. Part of the Greenham protest had always been that the military were occupying ground that should be open to everyone because it was a designated common ('common' land is land owned by the community not by an individual). Greenham is now a common again with a memorial to the Camp.

Greenham's legacy, however, is not just there on a patch of land, but in the lives of many individuals and organizations who campaigned for peace and justice over the following years. Its methods and even its style of building 'benders' were taken up in environmental protest camps. Its non-hierarchical method can be seen today in movements like UK Uncut, Occupy the London Stock Exchange camp and the 99% protest camps. While that legacy is not always recognized, it is powerfully present.

What about 'NUCLEAR'

By Joan Meredith

Women were very angry about Nuclear Weapons in the 1980s. The dropping of the atom bombs on Hiroshima and Nagasaki in the 1940s had left them in no doubt that civilisation faced a terrifying future if nuclear weapons were ever to be used again. Putting nuclear missiles on Greenham Common brought women together. Because of their protest the government was forced to remove them. The weapons were then placed on submarines based at Faslane in Scotland in the 1980s and 1990s. Angie Zelter, who, with a group of women had damaged a Hawker jet destined to bomb East Timor, decided it was time to protest again at Faslane. Direct action was to be used. The aim was to damage the submarines.

Greenham Common was so important. It laid the foundation for recent actions and many of the women who took part then, like Helen John and Sylvia Boyes, are still active today in anti-Nuclear protest groups. This includes Trident Ploughshares, a campaign to disarm the UK Trident nuclear weapons system in a non-violent, open, and peaceful way.

Women's Resilience through local activism / leadership

How much do you know much about your local community history of women's resilience?

Why not try and find out about key women in your area who have been rioters, rebels and change-makers?

Do any have streets named after them? Buildings or groups that carry their name? Or are they, like many activists, largely hidden from public view, but living in people's hearts and memories?

Try and find out about at least one of these women. You can do this by talking to people you know, asking in your local library or searching online.

The woman I have discovered is....

And this is a bit about her...

Women's resilience through politics

Diane Abbott
Born 27 September 1953

Dianne Abbott was born to Jamaican immigrants in London in 1953. Her mother was a nurse and her father a welder.

Diane went to Cambridge University where she studied History. It was here she first became involved in politics, working as an Administration trainee for the Home Office from 1976-1978. She then went on to be a Race Relations Officer at the National Council for Civil Liberties from 1978-1980.

Her career in politics really took off in 1982 when she was elected to Westminster City Council. She served there until 1986.

In 1987 she was elected to the House of Commons and became the MP for Hackney North & Stoke Newington.

Although she is a Labour MP, Diane has often challenged party policy. She voted against the 2003 Iraq War. She opposed ID Cards and campaigned against the government's plans to renew Britain's Trident Nuclear Weapons.

Her speeches have won awards for how they defend Civil Liberties.

In 2010 she stood for the Labour Party Leadership but was defeated by Ed Milliband. She continues to serve as an MP.

First Black Woman to be elected to the House of Commons in 1987

Illustration by Harriet Gibson

Women's resilience through politics

Claudia Jones
15 February 1915-
24 December 1964

Claudia Jones was born in Belmont, Port of Spain in Trinidad. She moved to New York City when she was eight years old. Due to poor living conditions, in 1932 she was struck with tuberculosis. The condition irreparably damaged her lungs and plagued her for the rest of her life.

In New York Claudia became an active member of the Communist Party. In 1941, at the age of 25, she became the National Director of the Young Communist League. In 1948 she became the editor of the 'Negro Affairs' column for the Communist party's paper.

She became a rousing public speaker on human and civil rights issues. She soon attracted the attention of the authorities and was imprisoned four times by the United States government. She was deported in 1955 because of her political activity and moved to England, where she was granted asylum.

Claudia moved to England at a time of heightened racial tensions. Many Afro-Caribbean people were violently attacked and in some cases, murdered. Claudia was instrumental in defending the Afro-Caribbean community.

She did this by making important and

Founder of the Notting Hill Carnival

lasting cultural contributions to Britain. This included the anti-imperialist, anti-racist paper, *The West Indian Gazette And Afro-Asian Caribbean News* that she founded in 1958. Her most famous legacy is the Notting Hill Carnival, founded in 1959. The event aimed to foster a spirit of community unity in the face of persecution. It continues to bring people from different backgrounds together today.

Illustration by Harriet Gibson

Women's resilience through politics

Indira Gandhi
9 November 1917–
31 October 1984

Indira Gandhi was born into the politically influential Nehru Family in India. Her father was Jawaharlal Nehru, a pivotal figure in the Indian independence movement and the first Prime Minister of Independent India. Indira gained the surname 'Gandhi' by her marriage to Feroze Gandhi. She had no relation to Mahatma Gandhi, either by blood or marriage.

In the 1930s, Indira spent time studying in England. She returned to India in 1941. In the 1950s, she served her father unofficially, as a personal assistant during his tenure as the first Prime Minister of India.

After her father's death in 1964 she became a member of Lal Bahadur Shastri's cabinet as Minister of Information and Broadcasting. After the sudden demise of Shastri, Indira was made Prime Minister. Gandhi soon showed an ability to win elections and outmaneuver opponents. She introduced more left-wing economic policies and promoted agricultural productivity. She was noted for her charismatic authority and political astuteness.

Indira was Prime Minister of the Republic of India until she was assassinated in 1984. She was in office for a total of fifteen years. In June 1984, under

The world's first and longest serving female Prime Minister

Gandhi's order, the Indian army forcefully entered the Golden Temple, the most sacred Sikh Gurdwara, to remove armed insurgents present inside the temple. She was assassinated in retaliation for this operation by her bodyguards. She was the first female prime minister to hold the office of Prime Minister and she remains the world's longest serving woman in this role.

Illustration by Harriet Gibson

Reclaim the Night

Reclaim the Night' or 'Take Back the Night' Marches began in the 1975. The marches captured the imagination of women from all over Europe and America. They helped raise issues about safety for all women both in the street, in the home, in the workplace and in the media. In 1977, women in the UK ran their own reclaim the night marches in response to the murders of women by the 'Yorkshire Ripper'. The actions were sparked by the advice given by the Police that women should just stay at home to avoid the risk of being attacked. Women said this was not good enough, and we have a right to walk the streets and be out at night without fear of attack or murder! Are we safe?

According to the British Crime Survey (2001) there are an estimated 47,000 rapes every year, around 40,000 attempted rapes and over 300,000 sexual assaults. Yet our tconviction rate is the lowest it has ever been, one of the lowest in Europe, at only 5.3%. This means that more rapists were convicted in the 1970s when Reclaim the Night marches first started than they are now. And lots of evidence suggests that many women do not report rapes when it happens to them, because they are frightened, feel ashamed, or don't think anything will happen if they do report.

Reclaim the Night Flyer from the Feminist Webs Archive

Most rapes are NOT committed by strangers (most survivors of rape know the person who raped them). But society builds up a fear about 'stranger danger' so many women are frightened of going out at night on their own just in case something happens to them.

As you stand

By Vanessa Fay

as you stand with your placard
looking down the line of women
   assembling from afar
all with a political cause
you stand tall
and smile

here
you are the embodiment of sixteen cartwheels
on a belly full of jelly and ice cream
you are raw with rare hope and dreams
anticipation, wonder

you are one strong unit in a rolling gamut of thunder
all different types of women uniting
   gathering momentum
as your confidence, somersaulting, strengthens
the street, for once, your landscape

here
you're free from the ache
at the crick of your neck
the constant check over each shoulder
here
you're not there
where you have to
run through the alleyway as quietly as possible
swift footprints hardly indenting the gravel
thankful that you made it through the route intact
despite the pure, pulsating fear
of what, or who, might be near

here, for once, you're one of the pack
shouting loud and proud
blowing whistles, hurling verbal missiles
       and chanting
the free spirit inside of you dancing
thinking: what if it was like this all of the time?
you could walk the roads on your own as a woman
and feel just fine, feel as though those pathways
       were rightfully yours
not eyes fixed to the floor, held breath, stiff neck
always half-aware of attack

and what's more, knowing that when you got back
you'd also be safe in your own home
have you ever typed 999 into your phone
just in case?
ever used your hands to shelter your face?
or if not, know at least one woman who has…?

but here
instead of being forced to take a cab
you can walk
and you will walk
in refusal of being scared and confined
you'll walk: tall, animated, alive.

Million Women Rise - NOW!

By Sam Aziz and MWR coalition

The Million Women Rise (MWR) Coalition is made up of a diverse group of individual women and women representatives from the Voluntary and Community Sector who are united by our outrage at the continued daily, hourly, minute-by-minute individual and institutionalised male violence enacted against women worldwide.

We believe that every woman and child has a right to live free from violence. That ongoing violence devastates not only the lives of the individuals directly affected but also the communities of which they are part. We have come together to organise a national demonstration against violence against women.

The Coalition has no formal or informal links to any particular or specific feminist or political networks. The Coalition is not partisan and brings together women who want to highlight the continuation of all forms of violence against women and demand that steps are taken to put an end to this.

MWR has a National Coordinating Group, which has overall responsibility for organising the march that takes place in London. Sub-groups work on different aspects of MWR such as fundraising, publicity and networking. There are local MWR groups around the UK. Check Your Area to find out what's happening in your city, town, and village.

Local MWR groups operate autonomously and encourage women to take part in the national demonstration as well as organising local events.

To conclude

As you have seen in this section, women can 'riot' in different ways.

Some women work within the system, entering politics and public life. Other women take more radical approaches such as marches, protests and breaking the law. Many women make small and important changes every day in their local communities, these women are part of our movement too, and vital to ensuring a better world for women.

" Courage

does not always roar, sometimes it is the quiet voice at the end of the day saying "I will try again tomorrow."

"

Mary Anne Radmacher

Pictures taken at Million Women Rise March 2010/2011 by Feminist Webs

Chapter 5 - ...Don't 'diet'

By Niamh Moore

I bet you have heard the words 'diet' and 'I'm on a diet' hundreds of times from women you know and seen 'diets' in almost every woman's magazine.

So when did the word 'diet' come to mean *not* eating, rather than a description of the foods we *do* eat?

How did calories become our main way of thinking about food – rather than how good food is for us? Calories seem such a 'thin' way of understanding food

A panel from 'My Body' Body image banner created by Feminist Webs 2009-2010

So, let's not go on 'a diet', but let's have a diet. Let's have an understanding of what we eat, and when, and how, and why and where it comes from.

There are so many questions to explore...

Food – our diet – after all, is one of the most important things that we have to nourish ourselves, and others, and the planet.

Food connects us with the world around us. Along with breathing in air, food is the other main substance we take in – and therefore what our bodies have to work with.

Food is social, cultural, biological, ecological, economic, emotional, historic, spiritual, ritual, habit, political, cyclical ... food is more than we can ever imagine.

There is an important book called *Diet for a Small Planet* – (note: it's not called diet for a small self/body) - written by Frances Moore Lappé.

There is an important book called *Diet for a Small Planet* – (note: it's not called diet for a small self/body) - written by Frances Moore Lappé.

What did she mean by 'a small planet'?

Well she didn't mean that we should starve the planet of the nutrients it needs, like some of us do to ourselves. She was one of many people pointing out that the way some of us eat means other people do not have enough to eat. For example, the USA and Europe are addicted to meat, sugar and dairy products. Producing these take a lot of the world's resources including land. This means there is not as much left over for the rest of the world.

Frances Moore Lappé said that some of the ways the growing and making of food is organised is in fact starving the planet. By small planet, she meant that everything is intimately connected: humans, animals, soil, water and air.

In the UK, most people buy their food

from supermarkets. Somehow, in the bright lights of the supermarket, it's easy to forget that it came from someplace else before that. We all know this, that it doesn't miraculously appear on the shelf, but it is all too easy to forget what we all surely know. How does this happen?

For instance, why do so many apples come thousands of miles like the USA or New Zealand? What's the nutritional value of this apple by the time we get to eat it? Is this kind of apple a day really going to keep the doctor away?

Hippocrates was a Greek man who is often described as the founder of modern medicine. He said: 'Let food be your medicine and medicine your food'. But what would happen if we went to the doctor and they prescribed an apple? (Not very likely, when so much about medicine today is about 'feeding' the pockets of rich businessmen who own pharmaceutical companies).

Feminists have reclaimed many words, perhaps too we could reclaim the word 'diet' – as the food we eat – not the food we don't eat.

Perhaps we should all have a diet? A diet for a small planet, a diet that looks after all of us: humans, other animals and the earth. We need a diet that can connect and nourish us. That helps us all to flourish.

Young women at the 2010 Feminist Webs launch in London next to 'My body' body image banner

Beauty

Beauty has always preoccupied women. But over the past two centuries, as women have gained more rights, the association of self-worth and appearance has intensified.

'There has been this enormous change from girls being principally concerned with good works to now being concerned with good looks as a measure of their self-worth,' says Joan Jacobs Brumberg, author of *The Body Project: An Intimate History of American Girls* and *Fasting Girls: The History of Anorexia Nervosa.*

Brumberg attributes the transformation in girls' behaviours to changes in technology, the coming of mirrors, modern hygiene, the rise of consumerism and popular culture. Attitudes towards attractiveness and ideals of beauty 'have changed drastically over the past centuries,' she says.

Key moments in Beauty timeline

1890s
Stage actress Lillian Russell is an ideal beauty, she is curvy and voluptuous and weighs about 200 pounds (14 stone).

1914
Mary Phelps Jacob invents the first American brassiere, made of lace. She patented the "Backless Brassiere" in 1914.

1918
Modern plastic surgery begins to grow as a profession. Surgeons trained to repair facial wounds in the first world war (1914-1918) go on to put their skills to work in private practice, on women's faces.

1921
The first Miss America beauty pageant is held in Atlantic City, New Jersey.

1950s
Black magazines like Ebony preach the advantages of lighter skin, which adds to the promotion of white skin as the ideal for black and white people to aspire to. (This happens at the same time as America has separate schools for white and black people, treating black people as second class citizens)

Training bras and girdles become common.

Marilyn Monroe epitomizes shifting beauty standards, with a change in focus from weight to large breasts.

1960s

Skirt hems rise and pants become acceptable for women.

To challenge the idea that only white skin is beautiful, the Notting Hill Carnival runs a contest to find the Caribbean Carnival Queen, and pioneers the 'black is beautiful' movement.

Dieting becomes popular. Weight Watchers is founded in 1963 in the USA, recruits 500,000 members and grosses $5.5 million in revenues. (It now runs in 30 countries worldwide)

1967

British fashion model Twiggy arrives in America weighing 91 pounds on a 5-foot-7-inch frame, triggering a shift in average sizes for fashion models.

1973

Our Bodies, Ourselves, is published by the Boston Women's Health Collective, encouraging women to take charge of their bodies and their health.

1977

Liquid-protein diets are banned temporarily after three deaths are reported during the decade.

1983

Singer Karen Carpenter dies at age 32 from anorexia nervosa, bringing eating disorders to America's attention.

1990s

For 15-30 year olds, 1 woman in every 100 suffer from anorexia. 1.6million people suffer from eating disorders in the UK. (www.disordered-eating.org.uk)

Our bodies are a battleground, what can we do?

By Laura Critchley

In Autumn 2009, Feminist Webs held a number of events for young women and their workers throughout the North West. These events took place in Halton, Wigan, Moston, Stockport and at the Water Adventure Centre in Droylsden, Tameside.

Each event was planned and delivered by young women and included sessions around body image and the media, animation and feminism. It provided inspiration for the people who went (including staff who learnt from each other).

Over 130 young women contributed ideas to a banner that spelt the words 'MY BODY' on a huge question mark. It was adorned with mutilated dolls and ideas about how we feel body image pressure from our friends and the media. The young women were annoyed that so many magazines air brush models and modify pictures to make people appear unrealistically thin. Some of the pictures have women in them with such thin waistlines and legs, that if these bodies existed in reality, these women would be too weak to stand up.

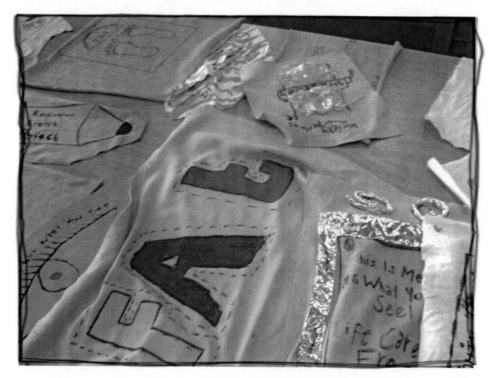

Making the body image banner 'My body' 2009-2010

We also created a booklet called 'post feminist', not because we thought we were beyond feminism but because it included loads of postcards from young women talking about their body image and what being a woman meant to them.

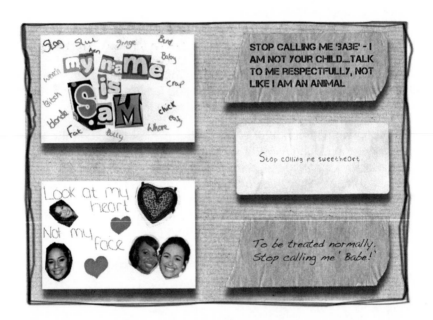

Post-Feminist book illustrating the views and opinions of young women across the North West

We also made an animation of how young women wanted to claim back natural beauty over the 'fake' ideas of how beauty is portrayed in the media.

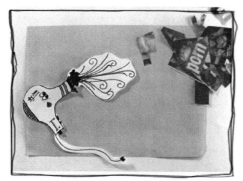

One participant said:

"" **Having** a negative body image drains all your confidence. ""

Still from 'More than a face' body image animation created 2009-2010 by Feminist Webs Young Women

The problem

From research we did:

- 48% of the women had low confidence in their own body image; (70% of these were young women or young volunteers)
- 8% had no body confidence (75% of these were under the age of 15)

The focus of our project was to help women understand where body confidence comes from and to boost their confidence in all areas of their life.

After the work we did young women were talking to each other more about body image, and were able to spot where unrealistic and pretend images of women were used by the media. Lots of the young women said they felt better about their body confidence as a result.

At a workshop in Preston with young and older women we looked at what pressures we face in our lives and where these come from

What Body image means to us

Too small

push up bra

Unique

Too big

Model

Glasses

Self Identity

Weight

contrived

I've got to be

unforgiving

Media

Shape

Pressure

Body Image

fear

Self-confidence

Boobs

hidden

pretty

attitude

Perfection

Make-up

Belly

fashion

Body Image workshop responses by Lucy and Jill from The Sparks Project

Having Body Confidence and feeling body pressures are NOT just about being sexually attractive to men:

Still from animation 'More than a Face' created 2009-2010 by Feminist Webs Young Women

As a lesbian I feel pressured into 'collecting tattoos' because some of my lesbian friends have loads of them. I also felt pressured into putting on weight to make myself seem tougher. Now as for my hair, I walked into my hairdressers and told them to do something, and it ended up with a funky very short spiky haircut. On the other hand, a young straight woman would be less likely to have tattoos, would probably want to slim down rather than fatten up, and would never allow a hairdresser to hack at their hair to make it so short and spiky!

Rachel, participant and volunteer

Draw here what positive body image means to you, perhaps focusing on the things you like about yourself and resisting the pressure to change yourself with cosmetics or surgery:

Draw or write here about your inner beauty:

What do you think when you buy a pair of shoes?
By Mary Kenny

What do you think about when you buy a pair of shoes? How fashionable they are, whether you can afford them and whether they'll go with your outfit? Do you ever think about how they might affect your posture, damage your knees and feet, increase your chances of getting a sprained or broken ankle, give you bunions and make it painful or difficult to walk (never mind run)?

For a lot of women the first three questions are the most important. There is nothing wrong with that except we don't seem to have a lot of control over what is fashionable. And what do you do if the fashion is harmful?

As you may have spotted, I'm talking about high heels here. And in recent years they have got extraordinarily high. In order to achieve a certain 'look' women wear shoes they cannot walk in. Film stars, TV presenters and models appear in the most fashionable and expensive footwear. They only have to stagger up a red carpet, across a studio floor or down a runway. Yet, real women (women who want to follow their fashion lead) usually have to think about catching the last bus home, and sometimes even in the snow!

Apparently, high heels make our legs look longer and our bums firmer. Er, so why do our bums and our legs need to look like that? The appalling truth is that women have always tolerated pain and risked their health (or put their daughters at risk) in order to be acceptable to society. In many cases this also means being attractive to men. Many women in China right up until the early 1900s had their feet 'binded' when they were young to keep them small and 'feminine'. As a result many of them suffered disabilities and found it hard to walk. We now look back on foot binding as a barbaric practice. Will we one day think the same about high heels? They have, after all, been associated with increased varicose veins, and a higher need for hip replacements in older life - not so different to foot binding!

I don't think there's anything wrong with wanting to look interesting, fashionable and attractive to potential friends and partners. What is wrong is women literally have to squeeze into narrow, controlling and damaging ideas of what attractive is.

But hey, Doc Martens and sports pumps are back in fashion. There's hope for us all!

Beth Ditto

Illustration by Amelia Lee

Beth Ditto and her band (The Gossip) wowed the world with their up beat and challenging song 'Standing in the Way of Control'.

Feminist, beautiful and voluptuous, Ditto is a great ambassador for larger women, and has modelled in high profile shows such as Gaultier's 2011 spring collection show. She challenges the media 'size zero' culture and shows that big is beautiful.

Endangered Species

In 1978 Suzie Orbach wrote a bestseller *Fat is a Feminist Issue*. Since then she has been one of the leading voices in Feminist Opposition to the media's campaign against women's natural bodies. She is active in the movement that tries to promote a positive body image for women. She campaigns against the media who tell us we can only be happy if we modify ourselves, go on a diet or buy their product to improve our natural looks. She did a number of international summits in 2011 called 'Endangered Species'. She suggested that women who truly love their bodies are an endangered species.

Resister sisters

by Vanessa Fay

disarmed, ready
with sisters
that I never had
we line in height order
disordered, manic, sad
and roar!
angrier than stomach pain

we are kettles reaching boiling
points
have no individual names
we are collected, packaged
the ground does not crumble beneath
our feet
instead, it is as if the earth itself
begins to beat
in time with our motions
for they may have stripped us
but never of our emotion
we are ravenous, feeling
thankful for this
we dance

dance like we have no other choice
we can dance
dance like it is our voice
expressive, loud, longing

outspoken
when we laugh
it is like the sun smacking the sky
diamond-knuckled
explosive expansive

our hope
silver succulent
frenzied vehement
our hands
wild, wicked?
we do not take orders
we thrash out
tumble, fall, whirl, whizz
swallow up whole their doubt
lights flash in our eyes

outspoken
we take one another's hands
tenderly
hold on with strength, ability,
spirit
none of us say it we just stand,
shoulders brushing

meanwhile, suits push keyboard
letters
write in standard English
what sounds wrong, harsh
splinters tongues
we are 'abnormal
sick, pained, insane'
we are 'not the same'

and yes, we outspoken
do not fit the shadows
we do not contort ourselves
instead, we bend
like spectacular fireworks
the embers of riots burning in our
chests

Good diets connect women and the land

By young and older women at the Resilience Residential 2011

Since time began people have talked about the Earth as a Mother, and some women have felt a spiritual connection to the land. Farming and growing our own food has often been important to women, who have been at the forefront of many 'Land Movements' and movements against deforestation. There are many of us today who buy our food not knowing how it was grown, or where it is from, but it hasn't always been this way. In the Second World War the 'Land Girls' were women who played an important role in the War effort by growing food to make sure the population had enough to eat.

Lots of women have also been very influential in the vegetarian movement including many suffragettes (the women who helped get votes for women). There are many reasons people become vegetarian, including because people do not want animals to die or live in cruel conditions. Some people even chose to become vegan instead, which is where people do not eat dairy (e.g. milk, cheese and eggs) or any other product made by animals (including honey). Other people believe that if we all cut down on our meat intake, and balance eating fish as well as meat, that this would be much more eco-friendly and would reduce Global Warming, and help save the world!

Why would you grow your own food?

By LIK:T

The Young women's health project (in Manchester), have had an allotment for the past 5 years. They grow their own food on the allotment and this is why:

"It's fun to go to the allotment and mix with friends and socialise, it has done a lot for my mental health"

"I would not usually eat vegetables, but once you have grown them yourself you are more likely to try them"

"Sometimes food can be quite expensive, but if you grow your own you can get it for free, even strawberries!"

Liz from the Young Women's Health Project digging carrots on a farm trip 2011

"I like being outside and digging. I used to have a garden and I miss it now, so it's nice to be able to come here"

How to grow your own food :

The Incredible Edible movement says that we can grow food in lots of places. Here are some ideas:

- If you have no outdoors space: Find a patch of waste ground, plant some seeds, plants or trees there (this is also known as 'guerrilla gardening'). If they survive and don't get stolen, keep going back to water them and eventually harvest the food! Or if this is too radical for you, see if there are local allotments that you can help out on or even rent your own one for a few pounds a year from your local council
- If you have a yard or balcony but no garden: get a big hessian sack and fill it with soil. Plant some old potatoes in it and watch them grow! You can also get small pots and grow carrots in them. Or with the help of a garden cane or two, you can grow beans or peas from in a pot
- If you have a garden: dig a patch and plant fruit, veg and herbs. Look online for tips, or buy a gardening book!

As fad 'diets' and clichés about beauty continually shape the way we feel about ourselves, it's time to say enough is enough. Eat well and balanced, exercise and take time for rest, never feel pressured to buy the latest thing or to change your body for your peers or for a partner. Go into the world wonderful woman, be healthy and be happy!

Chapter 6 - Freedom

This chapter is about how exciting our lives can be and the things we can do and think about that will make us free!

To begin we are going to look at learning. Yes, I know what you are thinking, you were expecting sky-diving and underwater exploring, or maybe a 'how to get out of jail guide' in the freedom section. Just run with this idea for a bit and ask yourself - 'what really gives us freedom?' What gives us the thoughts, the will and the means to be free? It all starts with learning.

Lifelong Learning
By Janet Batsleer and Margaret Beetham

Right from the beginnings of feminism, women and girls have fought for the right to be educated. To have an education lets women be free, to aim high and develop in the same way as their male counterparts.

For centuries, and still today in some places and communities, education for girls is viewed as less necessary than education for boys.

In the past girls were expected to learn subjects especially suitable to their role in life such as domestic skills. This included sewing, mending, laundry and ironing, cookery and childcare.

They were not encouraged to do subjects such as maths, science, carpentry and woodwork, electronics, plumbing, building or engineering.

It can still be hard for girls who want to do courses in traditionally 'boy' subjects. We still hear stories of girls being told that they cannot do plumbing, bricklaying or plastering because they will be 'the only girl in the class'.

Another aspect of feminism is recognising that women do have brains as well as beautiful bodies.

We all have the right to an education and to try to develop our abilities to their full potential. Many young women in the past felt they were limited by being taught how to make a pretty home or a pretty face, and not taught anything else. They felt they were more than just 'eye candy.'

You have never 'missed the boat' with learning...

If life stops you making the most of your talents and abilities when you are young, or if school turns you off; that doesn't mean you will never 'do anything' or 'be anyone.' You can carry on with or return to education, including University, at any age. And if you are the only girl or woman in the class, you can ask for support to keep on challenging the assumption that you should not be there. You deserve life long learning, it is the best gift you can ever give to yourself.

Exercise is freedom

To open this chapter we tfocussed on freedom of the mind. This can be gained through learning, education, art and dreaming. But what about freedom of the body? In part this is gained through healthy food and balanced diet (as we talked about in the last chapter) but it is also achieved through exercise. This might take the form of sky diving, walking, running, netball, rugby, playing on the Wii etc etc and yes, of course, one of our favourites - cycling!

Did you know that for more than a century, cycling has been seen as a very feminist thing to do? Why? Because women who cycle have a free mode of transport they can travel where they want to go and be self-reliant. You can travel through places you might not walk through, because you don't have to be afraid, you don't have to stop, you can just keep on cycling through to get where you want to go! So let's hear a little bit more about this cycling malarkey, and who best to lead us on this exciting tour than the women of the infamous Bicycle Dance troupe - The Spokes!

The Spokes guide to bicycle dance

We are a bicycle troupe. You may be thinking why do you dance with your bikes? It is because we aim to:

- Promote bicycle riding as sociable, more rewarding, more fun, less damaging to ourselves and the people and environment around us than this massive car culture
- We want to promote positive self image for people no matter what their body shape or appearance, and to celebrate the empowerment of women
- Encourage health and fun exercise that isn't in boring, expensive gyms
- Encourage people and ourselves to live out our craziest dreams every moment
- Have masses of fun and encourage others to as well!

How to start your own bicycle dance troupe:

1: Make a flyer advertising your bike dance troupe dreams and fix it to every bike you see to find some members for your bike dance gang!

2: Check out bicycle dancers from around the world on youtube, and get inspired by their dazzling moves.

3: Kids bikes are best for dancing, they're small so fit more easily into performance spaces, and you look funny riding them, bonus! Check out skips in your area to find some discarded kids bikes, or ask people you know with kids who might have old bikes.

4: Make a costume or pick a colour to unite your new bicycle dance troupe. And choose a bikey name for your troupe

5: Be silly and have fun with your new bike dance friends!

For more info or to contact us:
thespokes@lists.riseup.net
www.thespokes.wordpress.com

Let me tell you what I think of bicycling. I think it has done more to emancipate women than anything else in the world. It gives women a feeling of freedom and self-reliance. I stand and rejoice every time I see a woman ride by on a wheel...the picture of free, untrammelled womanhood

Susan B Anthony, US Civil Rights Leader, 1820-1906

The Spokes guide to how to fix a puncture:

What you'll need: 2 tyre levers, puncture repair kit, bike pump

1. Take off your wheel

You might need a spanner, or if you have a quick release fastening, flip it open and unscrew slightly to loosen. Careful not to lose the end! If the tyre is flat you won't need to un-do your brakes.

2. Take off your tyre on one side

Get one of your tyre levers, stick the flat end into the rim of the wheel (A) and hook it under the edge of the tyre. Then flip it down so the edge of the tyre pops out (B). You can hook the end of the tyre lever onto one of your spokes (C), or if it doesn't have a hook just hold it down.

Next take the second lever and do the same again (D), except this time you need to slide this lever away from the other (E), releasing the tyre from the rim as you go. It does takes a bit of force so don't be shy!

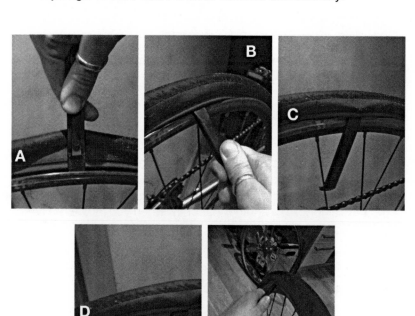

3. Pull out the inner tube

You might need to do some wiggling to get the valve out of the rim. Pump it up a bit to find where the puncture is, you might hear it hissing, or feel the air coming out. Some people stick it in a tub of water and look for bubbles.

4. Patch up the puncture

Some puncture repair kits come with glue and sandpaper. With these you sandpaper the area around the puncture to help the patch stick, then put some glue onto an area just bigger than the patch. Let it dry for a couple of minutes before sticking the patch on. Then push on the patch and hold in place for a couple more minutes till dry. Patience!

You can also get self-adhesive patches that stick themselves on, easy!

5. Replace the tube in the tyre

Nearly there! Tuck the inner tube back into the tyre, putting a little bit of air in can help the tube to stay in place, and prevent it twisting.

6. Tuck the tyre back into the rim

Push the tyre back into place in the rim of the wheel. As you work your way around the wheel, you may need to hold it in place with one hand to stop it popping out at the other end! Also watch out for bits of inner tube sticking out, they might cause another puncture when you inflate the tyre.

7. Put the wheel back on your bike and pump it up!

Secure the wheel tightly, and inflate the tube. Job done!

Whose resilience inspires us?

Here are some more wonderful 'Spirit Women' that we think capture the essence of freedom and the exciting life of being a woman:

Amelia Earhart
24 July 1897
disappeared 2 july 1937

Aviator and author

Amelia was born in Atchison, Kansas, USA. She had an unconventional upbringing since her mother did not believe in molding her children into 'nice little girls.'

Earhart saw her first plane when she was ten years old but it failed to interest her. It wasn't until 1918, when she saw a World War One pilot 'ace' doing a flying exhibition that she started to take notice of aviation.

On December 28, 1920, Earhart had a ride in a plane that would change her life forever. After that flight she became determined to learn to fly. Working at a variety of jobs she managed to save $1,000 for flying lessons.

From then Amelia did not look back. She was the first woman to receive the U.S. Distinguished Flying Cross, which was awarded to her for being the first woman to fly solo across the Atlantic Ocean. She set many other records, wrote best-selling books about her flying experiences and was instrumental in the formation of The Ninety-Nines, an organization for female pilots.

Amelia is perhaps most famous for her disappearance: in 1937 she attempted to make a circumnavigational flight of the globe. She disappeared over the central Pacific Ocean near Howland Island and was never seen again. We like to think she found a nice island and set up a wonderful feminist commune there!

Illustration by Harriet Gibson

Whose resilience inspires us?

Hope Powell
Born 8 December 1966

As a player Hope Powell had a successful career. She made her England debut at the age of 16. She won 66 caps for her country, playing mainly as an attacking midfielder. She scored 35 goals and acted as vice-captain. She played in England's first ever World Cup appearance in 1995.

At club-level, she played for Millwall Lionesses for nine years and won the FA Women's Cup three times, including a league and Cup double as captain of Croydon in 1996.

She was appointed the first ever full-time national coach of the England Women's Football team in 1998. During this time she led England to the 2001 European Championships, the quarter final of the 2005 European Championship and the final of the 2009 European Championship where they lost to Germany. She also led the team to 2007 and 2011 World Cup tournaments.

Hope is an 'A' License coach and in 2003 became the first woman to achieve the UEFA Pro License - the highest coaching award available. As well as coaching the England first team she also coaches at Under 15-21 levels.

Hope was awarded an OBE (2002)

England Women's Football Coach

and CBE (2010) in recognition of her contribution to developing the Women's game in England. In 2003 she was inducted into the English Football Hall of Fame, housed at the National Football Museum in Manchester.

Illustration by Harriet Gibson

Whose resilience inspires us?

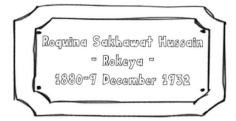

Roquina Sakhawat Hussain
- Rokeya -
1880-9 December 1932

Roquia Khatun was born in 1880 in the village of Pairabondh, Rangpur, in what was then the British Indian Empire and is now Bangladesh.

Roquia had two sisters and three brothers. Her eldest brother Ibrahim taught English and Bangla to Roquia and her sister Karimunnesa. Roquia's family looked down upon learning Bangla because many upper class Muslims of the time preferred to use Arabic and Persian to educate people. Both sisters later became authors.

Roquia married Khan Bahadur Sakhawat Hussain in 1896. He encouraged Roquia's study of Bangla and English and supported her interest in writing. He suggested that Roquia write in Bangla in order to communicate with lots of people. Her first essay was published in 1902, and her most famous work is the 1905 short story *Sultana's Dream*, an early example of utopian feminist science fiction.

In 1909, Sakhawat Hussain died. He had encouraged his wife to set aside money to start a school primarily for Muslim women. Five months after his death, Roquia established a high school naming it Sakhawat Memorial Girls' High School. The school is still running today and remains one of the most popular schools for girls in

Writer, Social Worker, Feminist

Calcutta.

Roquia also founded the Islamic Women's Association, which held debates about the status of women and education. She is one of the first Islamic feminists and argued that the traditions that oppressed Muslim women were not justified by the Koran, but were in fact misinterpretations of Islam.

Illustration by Harriet Gibson

Chapter 7 - Politically Correct or just plain correct?

" **If** I had a pound for every time someone said 'but what about the men' when we talked about the rights of women, I would be very rich. And if I had a pound for every time someone used the word 'Bitch' with no thought about the effect it has on our culture, I would be a millionaire "

Feminist Webs Participant, 2008

Sexist and non-sexist words and how to challenge them

By Ali Hanbury

Every day, every hour and sometimes every minute we are communicating with others. Often we do this using words. Some of us speak, sign, write, text and use internet messenger systems to talk with friends, family and relatives.

So do the words we use matter? Do we use different words to describe girls and boys, women and men? And if we do, why do we use different words, how do we use them and when? If I described a child as my **little soldier** would I be describing a boy or a girl? What if I called them my **little princess**?

These types of words continue into adult life too. For example, we use the words **'bird'**, **'slut'** and **'dear'** for women and **'lad'**,

Mud sticks - Anti-racism campaign poster in Feminist Webs Archive

'mate' and 'player' for men. The words we use help us build pictures in our heads. These pictures affect how we behave and help create the world we live in, and create the kinds of behaviour that is seen as being acceptable for women and for men. And these can be quite different depending on whether you're a woman or a man.

Are the words we use for different genders positive or negative? How can we start to think about, and get others to think about, the differences that these words can create between people (women, men and people who may not be either of these categories)? If you want to try this out, you could try by using some of the **bold** words mentioned above, but for the 'opposite' gender and see how people react! For example, calling a male partner your 'bird' or your little sister your 'little soldier'. This can help us and others to think about the words we use, how we use them, for who and whether or not they are fair.

This chapter explores what we value in terms of language and spaces, and challenges some of the things that people often 'accuse' feminists of.

To start let's be clear on what we mean by politically correct.

Political Correctness

Politically Correct was originally a term used by Communists in Russia in the early 1900s. It meant to do and say things that the Communist Party agreed with. If people were not politically correct they could face jail or other punishments. After the 1930s it stopped being widely used for a number of decades and people forgot its meaning.

In the 1980s, American Conservatives started using it to put down oppressed groups asking people to refrain from using hurtful language. The American Conservatives thought everyone should be allowed to use any language they like and accused people of being 'politically correct'.

Perhaps they thought that people being 'PC' (as it became known), was stopping people from talking about sensitive issues. Or perhaps they couldn't be bothered to think about the fact that not everyone was a straight, middle class, white man. If they had thought about this, they would realise that other groups didn't like being referred to in words that were offensive, objectifying, medicalised or colonial.

These conservatives were proudly 'politically incorrect' or 'not PC', and used whatever words they liked. This included words that were racist, sexist, able-ist, fat-phobic and homophobic. They said it was their right to use these words because it was about freedom of speech. They began to refer to things as 'PC' when those things challenged their right to say whatever they liked.

Many feminists believe that we SHOULD care about what we are saying, and use language thoughtfully.

Beyond Beijing - Image adapted from Beyond Beijing magazine in Feminist Webs Archive

It's not about being 'politically correct' it is about being considerate and intelligent.

By caring, we try to use words that currently cause less offence and upset to people.

These terms change over time. For example in race, the terms have shifted from 'coloured' to 'black' to 'black and minority ethnic' (BME) or 'people of colour'. Each of these words has its limitations, and has been discussed widely by people.

Some people think this is silly and makes it hard for people to talk about subjects because people get worried about using the 'correct terms', and think that they will use the 'wrong word'.

Other people believe that it is important to give the most accurate description of people e.g. 'coloured' refers to many colours and not to black or brown or yellow skin colour. 'Black' became the more common term, and held a political power, to unite people who were oppressed for not being 'white' , and to be able to fight for rights together.

When people say 'it's political correctness gone mad' they are usually referring to articles in the newspaper where a school has banned the word 'blackboard' or shopping centres ban shops putting up Christmas trees. The trouble is, these stories of 'banning' words or things are often more about hype than facts. There is not many instances where words have been 'banned'. It is strange that the media picks up on such stories when they ignore the fact that sexist and racist words are used every day by people and don't get challenged.

Think about what it means to laugh at political correctness. Is it just another way of saying, 'I can't really be bothered to be considerate to other people round me so I will just pretend that "things have gone too far" and that way I won't have to explain myself and why I remain a bigot?'

Perhaps inclusive language and political correctness are the same? They both

Illustration by Omena Osivwemu

aim to help us describe our world in a way that doesn't put people down or make the world un-equal or make groups of people invisible. Why use 'man hole cover' when 'drain cover' actually describes the object better? (After all, we are not describing something that covers a 'man's hole'). This also allows for the fact that a woman could go down the hole as part of their profession too, and doesn't assume that it is a 'man's job' to work in the water and sewerage industry.

Some words that put people down are illegal too, such as some words about race and sexuality. When these are used, anyone who hears them can report them as hate crimes, and those who say them can be punished for committing a crime.

A good way to think about what words to use is:

- Does the language used include words that put a group of people down and does this language cause offence?
- So if someone says 'faggot' and they are gay and they say it to another gay person, this **can** still be offensive, because it is a word people use to put gay people down, and gay people have a history of being persecuted in society
- If a word is used with the intention of being offensive OR the effect of the word being used causes offence, then this is where in some cases it is seen as a hate crime
- Does the word refer to a group in society that historically and currently are oppressed because of their identity e.g. Jews, Gay people, Black people, Disabled people, Women etc?
- If they are from a group that has less power in our society then it is even more important that we protect their rights, as these rights are more fragile than the rights of the powerful

Calendar made by Laurel St Young Women's Centre. The centre was originally set up in 1983 serving Norley Hall and Worsely Hall housing estates in Wigan. The calendar was donated to the Feminist Webs Archive by youth worker Marie Brookfield

Anti-discriminatory Practice - ADP

ADP is: action taken to prevent discrimination on the grounds of race, age, gender, disability, sexual orientation or religion. ADP promotes equality, fairness and ways of doing things that don't oppress people. If you want to be inclusive, the best type of language to use is called **'pro-social language'** which means it promotes inclusion, is anti-discriminatory, values diversity and does not come across as violent. This means avoiding stereotypes and abusive words, and asking people what words they use to describe themselves rather than presuming or labelling people.

If people are using words that are offensive, the best thing to do is not to attack them, but to work with them to understand the words and why they are using them. That way they don't feel silly and everyone can learn from the experience.

Try these in your own life:

1. **Paraphrasing** - if someone says 'He was acting like a spaz', you say, 'so you think he was acting in a silly way?' This way you are encouraging people to use other words that are less offensive, and subtly letting them know that you are not condoning what they said.

2. **Exploring and Questioning** - if someone says something that was a stereotype such as 'girls can't play football' try questioning their assumption. Ask them how they know this is true, if it is true and are there any examples that suggest this might not be true?

Can we reclaim language?

Language changes over time, and sometimes words start out with a positive meaning (e.g. Gay first meant 'Happy', then gay was used to refer to same sex love because it stood for Good As You 'G.A.Y'). Sometimes these words are then changed by dominant culture to become negative, (e.g. Gay is often used now to refer to things that people think are rubbish such as 'my Chemistry class is so gay'). Some people feel that you can make this work in the opposite way e.g. you can start using a once negative word and change it, so it now means a positive word. So for example, a disabled person might call themselves 'a cripple' and say it is ok for them to use it as they are 'reclaiming' that word. Examples of these in feminist movements include 'Ladyfest', 'Queer' and 'Slutwalks'. The purpose of these was to turn the stereotypes on their heads.

On the one hand you can see that this can be empowering for a group of people and help build up a sense of belonging, but on the other hand it might be hard to see how a group that does not hold the main power in society can 'reclaim' the word.

As Audre Lorde put it:

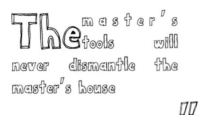

The master's tools will never dismantle the master's house

Audre Lorde, Sister Outsider

Sometimes people use words to describe themselves that other people find offensive. This is a good chance to learn from each other. Perhaps you could ask them:

1. Why have you picked that word?

2. What does that word mean to you?

3. Has that word been used against you/people you know?

4. Do you think you can reclaim negative words?

5. What impact does using that word have on yourcommunity, and on the wider world?

But why is language so important?

Our language shapes our thoughts which shapes our actions

Taken from Image Theory by Kenneth Boulder

Gordon Allport developed a scale of discrimation.

Allport suggests that through failing to challenge name calling and bad mouthing e.g **Level 1:** the words Bitch, slag, cow, ho, whore, people will become de-sensitised to discriminatory words, oppressive language and stereotypes.

Once assumptions, oppression and discrimination is accepted in language, be it verbal and/or written (e.g. SMS, graffiti, online), this may lead to an increase in discrimination.

Level 2: ignoring or excluding minority groups from activities (e.g. girls not allowed to play football alongside boys) then leads to...

Level 3: discrimination through action that directly or indirectly disadvantages someone else (e.g. not paying women as much as men, or believing that its a woman's job to cook and clean) then leads to...

Level 4: physical attacks and acts of violence (e.g. rape and domestic abuse) which can result in...

Level 5: murder or death (rape used as a weapon of war, and honour killings).

It is important to note that each of these levels of discrimination can also be directed to one's self and internalised. For example, using demeaning language to describe one's self can escalate to self-harm and suicide.

This scale can be stopped at level one. If we sort thing s out by the way we talk to people, we create safer, better places to live.

Handy hints when challenging discrimination, oppression and assumptions

- **A challenge should be seen as an invitation, not an attack**

Very few people would consider themselves prejudiced and would react negatively if accused of being so. Acknowledge that people's attitudes and statements may be due to their background and personal circumstances, and that the person may not realise they are being offensive.

- **Don't expect the world**

One challenge is unlikely to change a person's attitude. However, consistent challenging from everyone (including, people like family, colleagues and friends) will raise the awareness of an issue.

- **Address the attitude and/or the behaviour, not the person**

Attitudes and behaviours often change with experience and knowledge. Highlighting that a person's statement was discriminatory as opposed to claiming that someone is 'a homophobe' or 'sexist' is likely to result in a more positive response.

- **Stay calm**

Showing composure and calmness, as well as consideration for the other person's feelings, is more likely to allow for your message or challenge to get through. Shouting or getting frustrated may indicate a poorly thought-out view or uncertainty, and might just make them angry too. If you stay calm you can help them learn and grow.

Activity

It can be hard to think about how to challenge someone when they say something offensive. It may be helpful to plan your responses to common offensive words in advance. Try this activity below. Write down a word or phrase you have heard that is discriminatory in the first speech bubble, and write how you would challenge it in the second speech bubble.

Here is an example:

She is just being a right old bitch

Do you mean she is being nasty? Do you know where the word comes from? The word 'bitch' actually means a female dog. It is quite de-humanising to women, and is used more to refer to women than it is to men. Lots of people who are violent to women call women 'bitches' as a way to make them seem less human, and therefore easier to hit and abuse. So I would appreciate it if you thought about it a bit more.

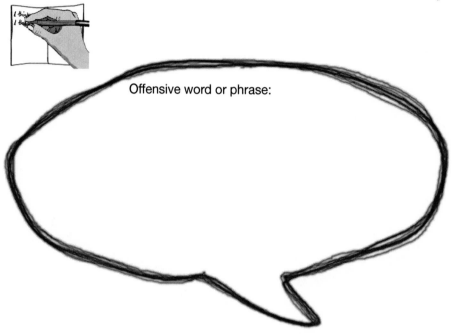

Offensive word or phrase:

How would you respond:

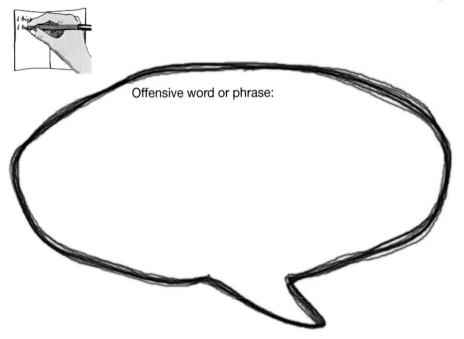

Offensive word or phrase:

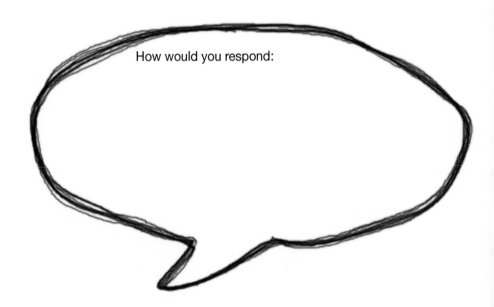

How would you respond:

This table helps illustrate which words are more inclusive and challenge sexism:

Problematic word or phrase	Meaning	Better word or phrase to use	Meaning
Man in the street	An average person but actually uses the word 'man' instead of a word for men and women	People or 'the average person'	Everyone, all genders
Lay man	A person who is not an expert, but the phrase uses the word 'man' instead of a word for men and women	Lay person/non-expert	Everyone who is not an expert, includes all genders
Man-made	Something created, but implies only men can create it	Synthetic, created, designed or made	Something which could be made by someone of any gender
Chairman/Foreman	Implies the senior roles must belong to men	Chair or Supervisor	The role could belong to someone of any gender
Manpower/Fireman/ Policeman	Implies that the work force only has men in it (and therefore a woman's place is in the home)	Labour force/staff/ workers/ fire fighter/ police officer	Jobs can be done by someone of any gender

Problematic word or phrase	Meaning	Better word or phrase to use	Meaning
Manning the stall	Implies that a man is doing it	Staffing	The stall can be staffed by someone of any gender
Forefathers	Implies that those from our past who influence us were all male	Ancestors	Implies that men and women have influenced our history, or people of other genders
Master copy	Comes from the word master for a man compared to mistress for a woman, which links paperwork/thinking to men rather than women	Original, top copy, main copy	More accurately describes the copy and its purpose. It doesn't need to have a gender

And can we mention something about 'Lady'?

...asked Viv, one of our feminist Webbers.

'What is a Lady?'- Hmm. People often think this is a polite way of saying 'woman' or 'customer' but really it suggests a certain type of behaviour from women. For example women must wear skirts, be polite, be passive and therefore need help and protection from men. Below is a combination of what some dictionaries have to say about the word:

 Lady - noun

1. A woman regarded as proper and virtuous

2. A well-behaved young girl

3. A woman to whom a man is romantically attached

4. Informal 'A wife'

5. Used as the title for the wife or widow of a knight or baronet

6. Used as a form of address for a marchioness, countess, viscountess, baronetess, or baroness

7. Used as a courtesy title for the wife of a younger son of a duke or marquis

So why not start using the word 'Woman' instead? This is a word which does not create such a stereotyped visual picture of a woman. Or if that doesn't float your boat, then create a word or find a word that works for you, and tell everyone you meet about your new word every time they start to call you 'lady'.

Activity

Now go back to the list in the table on page 136-7 and see if you can make up new words which you think are even better than those suggested!

Now try some of your own (we have put in a few suggestions to get you started):

Problematic word or phrase	Meaning	Better word or Phrase to use	Meaning
Girl (when referring to adult women)			
Guys (when referring to a mixed gender group)			
Craftsmen			

Whose resilience inspires us?

Audre Lorde
18 February 1934 -
17 November 1992

Audre Lorde was born in New York City. Her parents were Caribbean immigrants from Grenada. She graduated from High School and after the death of her close friend, she immediately left her family. She went to Hunter College and gained a Bachelor degree in Library Science and supported herself with a range of jobs.

At this time she started exploring her lesbian sexuality. She spent a year at the University of New Mexico where she affirmed her identity as a lesbian and a poet. She then returned to New York.

Writer, Poet and Activist

Audre's poetry began to be published in the 1960s. Later collections included Cables to Rage (1970) and The Black Unicorn (1978). Her poetry explored mythology, sexuality and racial politics. Audre became the State Poet of New York from 1991-1992.

Audre also wrote her life story in creative ways. *Zami: A New Spelling of My Name* (1983) was a 'mythography' and *The Cancer Journals* (1980) told the story of her battle with breast cancer. She is also renowned for her critical writing and political speeches. Many of these are documented in the collection *Sister Outsider* (1984).

Audre made important criticisms of heterosexual, middle-class, white feminism. In particular she challenged the assumption that all women had the same life experiences. Audre pointed out that there are many differences between women because of race, class, sexuality, age and disability. While differences need to be acknowledged by any political feminist movement, she also asserted these differences are a source of celebration.

Illustration by Harriet Gibson

Understanding why some space are women-only

By Amelia Lee

I remember finding out about the Pankhurst Centre who have a women-only space, and thinking, why women only?

My first thought was - isn't that sexist?

Ten years on from then, and after much reading and thinking- here's why I think it can be a very good idea.

1. It is not sexist.

Do you hear people saying how bad it is that able-bodied people are not allowed along to the disabled people's group? Do you hear adults complaining that they are not allowed in a youth club?

Probably not. And that is because sometimes it is fine for people to form a group with people who share a common experience.

It is also not sexist to have women-only spaces because sexism is about power, and the power of society has been with men for centuries. Male language, male jobs, working men's clubs, mankind, men in parliament and men with the vote. Women have been excluded because of male power and systems that privilege men over women. This has been described as **patriarchy.** Women-only spaces give women the chance to take back power and make decisions for ourselves.

Women want to claim for themselves the power to assemble together, for self-determination and voice.

To call this 'sexist', neglects the reality of power differences between the sexes and ignores the reality of male privilege.

2. Sometimes people need a women-only space to really speak about things, or to be heard.

This may be the case when talking about experiences such as domestic abuse.

Years of subtle psychological conditioning can potentially still cause women to react defensively to the presence of men.

Women can find it easier to speak honestly about their experiences of sexual and physical violence in women-only groups.

Women's Rights Cartoon by Lucy Gibbs for the LIK:T Magazine 2007

The 'Gender in the City' research in Manchester also found that even where women and men were together in equal numbers in meetings, it was more common for men to speak than women. It was also found that women's ideas were not written down in the minutes of the meetings as much as men's.

" **When** a man gets up to speak, people listen, then look. When a woman gets up, people look ; then, if they like what they see, they listen **"**

Pauline Frederick

3. Sometimes it is necessary to make a point

Reclaim the Night (RTN) marches and protests are about women reclaiming public spaces at night. They are about women feeling safe and being able to walk in public spaces. Having men marching alongside women can imply that women need to protection of some 'nice' men against other 'dangerous' men in order to be safe on the streets at night. This obviously does not make sense as the point of marching is that we don't need a man to walk us home. The streets should be safe enough for women AND men to walk them.

" **RTN** in Brisbane have always encouraged men simply to line the streets to show support - one of the points of RTN is that women do not need male protectors to walk the streets at night. If men march it would defeat the purpose! But seeing men - usually the men in women's lives - on the sideline showing support is great, because if anything it shows that men can actually respect women's only spaces **"**

Some Reclaim the Night Marches have decided to have joint marches with men and women, so that men can more actively support. The decision is up to each group, and there is not a right or wrong approach. They most important thing is that the decision but must come from women themselves, following informed discussion and not because they feel pressured into including men, even by other women

4. Sometimes services meet a particular need for women that the mainstream general services do not, e.g. well women clinics

Why Women? Campaign findings 2007 (Women's Resource Centre) found that 97% of women they surveyed thought a woman should have the choice of accessing a women-only support service e.g. if they had been the victim of a sexual assault.

56% of the women surveyed would choose a women-only gym over a mixed gym, 28% of women would choose to go to a mixed gym, 16% didn't know.

Of the 560 women that would chose a women-only gym, they cited reasons such as: feeling more comfortable, less self-conscious and less intimidated. Respondents stated that they didn't want men watching them, looking at their bodies or sexually harassing them.

90% of women polled believed it was important to have the right to report sexual or domestic violence to a woman (such as a woman Police Officer); 87% thought it was important to be able to see a female health professional about sexual or reproductive health matters; and 78% thought it was important to have the choice of a woman professional for counselling and personal support needs.

5. Trans women have rights, and responsibilities too

Trans women are women who were assigned male at birth, e.g. had male biology (eg. genitals) when they were born, and have transitioned into becoming a woman (sometimes through clothing, voice, name change and also sometimes – though not always - through surgery).

Trans women have the right to be included within feminism and feminist struggles? The experiences of being trans means that often trans women have faced a lot of exclusion and persecution from others. If we want to be inclusive and not oppress people, then trans women should have the right to trans spaces, mixed spaces and to occupy women-only spaces.

To conclude - women have the right to women-only spaces

Committed male feminists must learn to overcome the personal feeling of rejection or 'discrimination' that may come along with women's-only spaces. They must learn to respect women's decisions to create those spaces where necessary, and understanding that is vital for wanting true equality.

"

As all advocates of feminist politics know most people do not understand sexism or if they do they think it is not a problem. Masses of people think that feminism is always and only about women seeking to be equal to men. And a huge majority of these folks think feminism is anti-male. Their misunderstanding of feminist politics reflects the reality that most folks learn about feminism from patriarchal mass media.' Bell Hooks Feminism is for Everybody - 2000

"

Audre Lorde, Sister Outsider

Chapter 8 - Peace Sister

This chapter looks at peace as something we want and not what we have. Violence is a daily experience for many women around the world, who live in fear from domestic abuse. Women also suffer in wars in many parts of the world, including through gendered forms of violence, such a rape being used as a weapon of war. We take a look at what we can do, as women, to challenge violence in all its forms, and achieve something we all deserve: peace sister!

Resilience to violence

By Joan Meredith, Alison Ronan and Niamh Moore

In the 1970s the Women's Liberation Movement had to take matters into their own hands as domestic violence was not a priority of male dominated governments. Women like Helena Kennedy (*The Bar on Trail* 1978), Erin Pizzey (*Scream Quietly or the Neighbours Will Hear* 1974) and Susan Brownmiller (*Against our Will* 1975) were alerting the public to domestic violence issues through their books. Women, against all the odds, got together and established refuges, womens centres and Women's Aid as places where women could at last feel safe.

In 1984, Prime Minister Margaret Thatcher was forced to hear evidence about of the reality of violence against women, and was shamed into hearing evidence from Welsh Women's Aid and Rape Crisis. At last, the Government was taking notice. Domestic violence was beginning to be taken seriously by the courts and police, and was recognised as a criminal offence. The refuges empowered women of all classes to talk to each other and do something about their situation.

Image created by Brinnington Young Women

Whose resilience inspires us?

Zora Neale Hurston
7 January 1891 –
28 January 1960

Zora was born in Notasulga, Alabama in 1891. When she was three her family moved to Eatonville, Florida, the first all-Black town to be incorporated in the United States. She always felt Eatonville to be her proper home, and describes it in her 1928 essay 'How It Feels to Be Colored Me'.

In 1918, Zora started undergraduate studies. At one college she was the sole black student. She graduated with a degree in Anthropology in 1927 at the age of 36. Hurston traveled extensively in the Caribbean and the American South and immersed herself in local cultural practices to conduct her anthropological research. She published this work in the collection *Go Tell My Horse* (1938).

Zora was part of the Harlem Renaissance, an African-American literary movement in the 1920s that included other prominent African-American writers such as Langston Hughes and Wallace Thurman. They published novels, short stories and articles in defiance of the racist discrimination they experienced in American society.

It was in the 1930s when Zora was most prolific. She published three novels including *Their Eyes are Watching God* (1937), now widely regarded as

Folklorist, Anthropologist and Novelist

a literary classic. The book brought to the life experiences of black women to the attention of popular culture. Towards the end of her life, the media largely forgot Zora. Later, great African-American women writers such as Alice Walker and Toni Morrison cited her as an inspiration to them.

Illustration by Harriet Gibson

Violence against Women

by Jo Lane

Violence against women (from men) is one of the biggest human rights abuses of our time. Worldwide it is estimated that Violence against women causes more deaths and disabilities amongst women aged 15-44 than traffic accidents, malaria, cancer and war (World Bank discussion paper 225, 1994).

The issues that affect women can include domestic abuse, forced marriage, rape and sexual violence, sexual harassment, female genital mutilation, trafficking and sexual exploitation, and crimes in the name of honour. The most common form of abuse experienced by women globally is committed by a man that the woman is in a close relationship with. This is called 'Domestic Abuse.'

Domestic abuse, also sometimes called relationship abuse, is when one person hurts or bullies another person who is their partner, was their partner or who is in the same family. It can include physical, emotional, sexual or financial abuse.

Statistics for the UK show:

- 1 in 4 women will experience some form of domestic abuse in their life-times
- 54% of UK rapes are committed by a woman's current or former partner
- Every 34 minutes a rape is reported to the police in the UK

Women's Aid

Women's Aid is the key national charity working to end domestic violence against women and children. They support a network of over 500 domestic and sexual violence services across the UK. These services provide confidential advice and support for women who are experiencing abuse, and refuges that provide a safe place for women if they need to flee.

 Survivor - *Noun*

1. A common word for women who have experienced domestic violence is 'survivor'. This word if often used instead of victim, because 'to survive' is a more hopeful term and focuses on the future

The website - www.womensaid.org.uk offers advice and guidance for survivors, professionals and the general public. The website also features a downloadable survivor's handbook available in many different languages. This offers in-depth advice about finances, housing, civil law options and advice on how to keep safe. The publicity featured on the next page is from Manchester Women's Aid and displays the Manchester Women's Aid number, but it does also provide the National domestic violence 24-hour free phone number (run in partnership between Women's Aid and Refuge).

Ticket to healthier relationships:

A healthy relationship is when two people treat each other as equals, they trust each other and treat each other with respect.

Freedom: Being able to live your life free from violence, intimidation or threatening behaviour and make choices for yourself.

Healthy relationships are possible and everyone deserves to be in one

manchester
women's aid

Free 24 hour Domestic Violence Helpline
0808 2000 247
If you experience violence, sexual or emotional abuse in your relationship or from a close family member please call this number for help and support.

0161 6607 999 Mon-Fri / 9-5pm
In an Emergency always call 999

Organisations like Women's Aid can help to keep you safe. Your safety is paramount to being able to lead an exciting and fulfilling life.

Other useful contacts:

Southall Black Sisters is a not-for-profit organisation established in 1979 to meet the needs of black (Asian and African-Caribbean) women. Their aims are to challenge violence; empower; and help women assert their human rights to justice, equality and freedom. It is based in London. **Helpline 0208 571 0800** (not 24 hours)

Rape Crisis (England and Wales) campaign to raise awareness of the prevalence of sexual violence. They highlight the importance and need for appropriate, high-quality and specialised support. Rape Crisis Centres provide lots of support in many ways, and are a valuable resource that not enough people know about. www.rapecrisis.org.uk **Freephone helpline 0808 802 9999** (not 24 hours)

Forced marriage

Karma Nirvana Forced Marriage **Helpline - 0800 5999 247** The helpline runs from 9am to 9pm 7 days a week, 365 days per year. Karma Nirvana is a registered Charity that supports victims and survivors of forced marriage and honour based abuse. The words Karma Nirvana simply mean 'Peace and Enlightenment' as this is the aim of the organisation.

The forced marriage unit offers confidential advice and assistance for those at risk of being forced into marriage **020 7008 0151 (or 0044 20 7008 0151** if you are overseas)

Trafficking

STOP (Trafficking UK) is a charity working to support trafficked people and raise awareness of the urgent problem of modern day slavery in the UK, which affects thousands of women. www.stop-uk.org

credit needed

16 Days of Action

Look out for the 16 Days of Action to end violence against women. This runs every year from 25th November (the International Day For Elimination Of Violence Against Women) up to the 10th December (International Human Rights day). Men and women, organisations and individuals, all stand together to raise awareness, campaigning to end violence against women. There are various events held nationally for people to get involved in. You could also choose to go a step further and create your own event!

When it is easier to convict the guilty for robbery than for rape, is something in society conspiring against us?

Conviction rates for rape remain very low (5.7%), and this is a huge problem for our society. Helena Kennedy QC in *Eve Was Framed: Women and British Justice* highlights that we need more women in senior legal roles such as Judges and QCs, and we need to look at how to make reporting and prosecuting less traumatic for the victims of rape.

Helena Kennedy and others argue that we need to be proactive in addressing how survivors of rape are treated, and ensure that there is a higher conviction rate for rape. . We need specialist teams of trained people to support women. We need to build up examples of what works and share this. Not just across the UK but throughout the world.

It is no answer to make a simple call for equal treatment. Dealing equally with those who are unequal creates more inequality

Helena Kennedy - Eve Was Framed, Vintage, 1992, p.31

In no other crime is the victim subject to so much scrutiny at trial, where the most likely defense is that the victim consented to the crime. The Home Office recognizes a 'justice gap' in the reporting and conviction of rapes and we need a review of judicial systems and education of judges to address this failure in our courts

Bristol Feminist Network, 2011

No-one has the right to hurt me
Julie Tweedale and Elaine Howard, Freedom Personal Safety

At Freedom Personal Safety specialists, we teach women moves and techniques to stop someone hurting them. But staying safe is as much a state of mind as it is about punching and kicking.

Reducing risks and avoiding situations that make you feel vulnerable is key to 'self defence'. We hope the women we teach never have to use the physical techniques they learn, but if they do, we want them to feel empowered and to use their inner and physical strength to resist an attack.

Communication is an important aspect of personal safety.

Think about what you say, how you say it and most importantly, your body language. What does it say about you? Do you look aggressive, passive or assertive? Men who attack women are like playground bullies – they want someone they can dominate to make themselves feel powerful and 'in control'.

They are looking for women who look vulnerable and like a 'victim'. Someone who won't fight back or attract attention. You can do a huge amount to keep safe just by walking confidently, making eye contact (but not staring aggressively), as well as appearing calm and in control.

Most women will experience unwanted attention from men and as many as 1 in 3 women will be sexually assaulted or raped in their lifetime. Many women believe that they are to blame for attacks or sex crime committed against them. They are not to blame: Getting drunk, wearing revealing clothing or getting intimate with someone is not a crime. Rape and sexual assault is.

Physical defence moves

These moves are part of a basic physical defence course for women, developed by R.A.D Systems in the USA. The techniques are designed for 'everywoman' regardless of your size, fitness, agility or age.

Some basic principles:

- Maintain eye contact so an attacker knows you are not a 'victim'
- Shout 'NO' each time you make a move or strike. This will attract attention but also sends an important message to your attacker that what they are doing is wrong and that you are going to stop them
- If you choose to strike them with a punch or kick ensure your strikes are focused on his vulnerable areas (nose, groin - penis/testicles - foot etc.) and that you repeat them until you get the chance to escape
- If you decide to physically defend yourself, you may get hurt with cuts, bruises and even fractures, but this is likely to be less damaging than being abused

The moves and descriptions below have been included to give you an idea of what you can do if you are attacked. It is important that you learn how to use your 'personal weapons' and harness your strength effectively. This should be done face-to-face with an instructor. We strongly recommend that you learn some basic physical defence with a trained instructor, but the basic moves here are a first good step.

Defensive stance

This is the defensive stance you can use if someone tries to attack you:

Punch

This is away to punch someone who is attacking you, and at the same time, put your other hand up to block any punches or slaps from them.

Sweep Kick

Bring your back leg forward and swing your foot towards the groin. Bend from the knee and maintain eye contact. If you can't reach the groin, aim for the shin. Shout 'NO!'

Photographs by Sandie Nicholson

Staying safe tips

- Strong, confident body language and making eye contact is assertive behaviour which may help you stay safe
- Always be prepared when you go out, especially at night – e.g a fully charged mobile phone and cash if you need to get a bus or taxi home
- Avoid walking alone, especially at night. Why not cycle instead? If you do go home on your own, why not text a friend to let them know you got home safe and they can do the same with you?
- Trust your instinct. If you feel that something or someone is making you feel uncomfortable, decide how to respond. Don't ignore this feeling – act on it
- Be aware of your surroundings when you are out and about, for example, stick to places that are well lit rather than taking a short cut through a dark park
- Walk briskly, with confidence. Look alert, be alert. Don't use your mobile phone when you are out on your own unless you have to
- If you feel you are being followed, change direction. Go immediately to an area where there are people about (if possible)
- If you do need to defend yourself physically, drop whatever you are holding and make the most of your personal weapons (hands, feet, elbows, knees, voice)
- Identify his vulnerable locations (groin - penis/testicles - face, feet, lower arm, shin, stomach etc)
- When you make a strike, make it clean, strong and powerful and repeat it until you can escape
- Give a full description to the police as soon as possible
- **Remember: no-one has the right to hurt you and if someone does try to hurt you. It is okay to try and stop them**

Freedom Personal Safety is a non-profit-making organisation dedicated to empowering women and children to keep themselves safe. www.freedompersonalsafety.co.uk

Women's resilience to war

By the Resilience
Residiential
Participants

- Who is involved in war?
- Who begins wars and who suffers from war?
- How have women's experience and suffering during war been sidelined or made invisible?
- How have women been involved in challenging war, creating peace, and processes like in conflict resolution? (e.g.Naomi Tutu who championed peace and reconciliation projects in South Africa)

Women have been involved in anti-war protests throughout history, including the First World War in 1914-18. In Manchester there were young women who were active in the 'No Conscription Fellowship', the small campaign to stop the Government making young men go to war. They supported the men who didn't want to fight. These men were called conscientious objectors and were sent to prison. They also set up a local branch of the Women's International League and planned lots of demonstrations under the banner of the Women's Peace Crusade to try and get the war to end.

I don't believe that the big men, the politicians and the capitalists alone are guilty of the war. Oh, no, the little man is just as keen. Otherwise the people of the world would have risen in revolt long ago! There is an urge and rage in people to destroy, to kill, to murder, and until all mankind, without exception, undergoes a great change, wars will be waged, everything that has been built up, cultivated and grown, will be destroyed and disfigured, after which, mankind will have to begin all over again. It's really a wonder that I haven't dropped all my ideals, because they seem so absurd and impossible to carry out. Yet I keep them, because in spite of everything, I still believe that people are really good at heart

Anne Frank

Whose resilience inspires us?

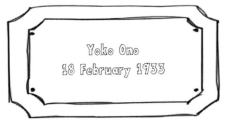

Yoko Ono
18 February 1933

Yoko was born in Japan but spent the first ten years of her life moving back and forth between the United States and her homeland. Her father was a banker and had to move a lot because of work. In Tokyo she experienced the devastation of the Second World War and her father was imprisoned in a Prisoner of War camp. After the war Yoko's family moved to New York where they settled. At this time Yoko became interested in the radical art movements that were taking place in the city. She married twice, both of which ended in divorce.

In the 1960s Yoko started to display her art that was often conceptual, participatory and performance based. She was part of a number of people who questioned what art meant, what it could be and what it was. An example of her conceptual art is the book *Grapefruit* (1964). The book contains short instructions, and formed the basis of many of Yoko's performances throughout her career. She also made a number of experimental films during the 1960s and 1970s.

Yoko is of course famous for her relationship with John Lennon from The Beatles. The pair collaborated on art projects, including their week long Bed-Ins for World Peace. They also made number of recordings together in the

Artist, Musician, Peace Activist, Visionary

1970s including the song 'Give Peace A Chance' and numerous albums. Yoko has also made a number of albums in her career, and she is an exceptional songwriter. This includes *Season of Glass* (1981), *Yes, I'm A Witch* (2007) and many others.

Yoko's varied art career has been recognised by large retrospective exhibitions all across the world. She has won awards and honorary degrees. She continues to create and spread her message of peace and love in many different, inspiring ways.

Illustration by Harriet Gibson

What can I do about ending violence?

There are lots of things you can do to help end violence. You can talk to and support your friends. You can volunteer your time with a domestic abuse helpline. Don't worry if this seems daunting because free training is always given. Or you can write letters to the government on behalf of a local group asking for better laws and procedures about rape. You can also join some of those women mentioned in the Chapter 4 who campaign against war, such as the anti-nuclear organisation Trident Ploughshare.

You might also want to work with men or the wider community to help end violence. Here are examples of organisations that do this:

Mothers Against Violence - MAV -

by Patsy and the other mothers

Since August 1999, Mothers Against Violence (MAV) have supported the inner city communities of Greater Manchester. MAV was birthed at a time when gun violence was at it worst in inner city Manchester. Three young black males were murdered in the space of eight days in one area. The mothers of that community took a stand and came out fighting. Not with guns, but with words of Hope. The women had a meeting and decided to do something. It is with this same hope that Mothers Against Violence now serves the community providing mentoring support, educational awareness of gun and knife crime, counseling, workshops, and outreach work which includes campaigning for positive change in our community.

The Alternatives to Violence Project - AVP

The Alternatives to Violence Project is a vibrant national charity run by a large group of dedicated volunteers. Our trained volunteer facilitators offer workshops in the community, in prisons and in other settings.

Conflict is part of life and there are ways of handling it well. In our workshops, participants draw on their own experiences to explore the conflicts within their lives and find ways of dealing with them.

Many of our participants have histories of both using and suffering from physical violence. Others come to AVP simply to build better relationships and to communicate well in heated situations. Everyone is welcome.

and finally...

Remember that challenging violence against women is everybody's job. Lots of violence happens in the home, and by people we know. If we work together and support each other we can change things. Look after one another and be patient if you are helping someone come to terms with violence they have faced.

Chapter 9 - The Art Part

by Sally Carr - with thanks to Linda Nochlin

As you have already seen in the book, through the music of the Riot Grrrls or the paintings of Alison Lapper, art plays an important and central place in our lives as women. It helps us understand and celebrate the world around us and challenge it.

It was through the fiction and non-fiction books of the 1960s and 1970s that many women in the UK and beyond became aware of some key issues effecting women. Reading books empowered women with knowledge and inspiration to change the world.

Freedom Cup cake made by young women

Many women have used art to challenge the system. Many people have used art, such as cartoons and illustrations, to make feminists and women's rights seem silly, misguided or dangerous, and have tried to take power away from women.

Through visual art, music, books and popular culture women have sometimes been celebrated and often been invisible. The art world still remains ruled mainly by men. Crafts, for example knitting and cooking, are not regarded as 'fine art'. Yet many women have a history of making craft in the home, teaching their children through art, and helping make the world beautiful and meaningful.

How has art shaped women's lives?

Why Have There Been No Great Women Artists?

Women artists have been involved in making art across history and across continents. Textile arts have often been associated with women. However who makes art changes in different cultures and communities. Many art forms dominated by women and indigenous cultures have been historically dismissed as 'craft'. Whereas the category of 'fine art' (made by men), has been held in high esteem.

Women artists have always faced challenges due to gender biases in the mainstream fine art world. They have often encountered difficulties in training, traveling and trading their work, and gaining recognition.

This is largely down to excepted ideas of what men and women 'should' do.

Art historian Linda Nochlin (in 1971) wrote the essay *'Why Have There Been No Great Women Artists?'* It explores in great detail the field of art history, where the white Western male viewpoint has been unconsciously accepted as *the* viewpoint of the art historian, to the exclusion of women artists. She highlights:

'But in actuality, as we all know, things as they are and as they have been, in the arts as in a hundred other areas, are stultifying, oppressive, and discouraging to all those, women among them, who did not have the good fortune to be born white, preferably middle class, and above all, male.'

The fault lies not in our stars, our hormones, our menstrual cycles, or our empty internal spaces, but in our institutions and our education (education understood to include everything that happens to us from the moment we enter this world of meaningful symbols, signs, and signals). The miracle is, in fact, that given everything against women, that so many have managed to achieve so much sheer excellence, in science, politics, or the arts.'

Women's art in the middle ages

Let us start our journey to understanding the great, nameless and invisible women artists from history, with one of the most famous works of art in the world, the Bayeux Tapestry.

The Medieval tapestry of cloth embroidered with wool is 70 metres long. It narrates the Battle of Hastings and the Norman Conquest of England. The Bayeux Tapestry may have been created in either a commercial workshop, by a royal or aristocratic lady and her servants, or a workshop in a nunnery, such as the 14th century royal workshop based at the Tower of London.

This world renowned and historically significant piece of art is never referred to as craft, and this may indeed be because of whom and what it depicts: male endeavours and power.

Stockport Banner, 1936

Only three women are shown on the main narrative of the Tapestry

Stop press! Women call for society to finally notice women's art

At around the same time as Nochlin's essay in the 1970s, feminist artists and art historians came together to create a Feminist Art Movement. It overtly addressed the role of women in the art world and explored women in art history.

In the 1980s, women making art plus the concept of who was shown/depicted in art became a central campaign of the American feminist artists know as the Guerrilla Girls.

Guerilla Girl - inspired photo

Starting in 1985, a group of women artists protested outside The Museum of Modern Art in New York. The museum opened an exhibition entitled 'An International Survey of Painting and Sculpture'. This was supposed to be an up-to-the minute summary of the most significant contemporary art in the world. Out of 169 artists, only 13 were women. All the artists were white, either from Europe or the USA.

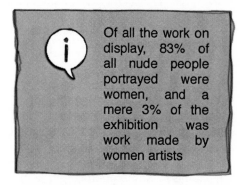

Of all the work on display, 83% of all nude people portrayed were women, and a mere 3% of the exhibition was work made by women artists

In an interview, one of the Guerrilla Girls said: 'That was bad enough, but the curator, Kynaston McShine, said any artist who wasn't in the show should rethink "his" career. And that really annoyed a lot of artists because obviously the guy was completely prejudiced.'

What the Guerrilla Girls discovered about who was depicted in the exhibition was even more alarming: most of the women in paintings and sculptures were naked.

It led the Guerilla Girls to ask: Do women have to be naked to get into a museum in the USA?

It is becoming clear that so-called 'great' art in history is made by men. This is not because men are better artists than women, but because men had the access to the opportunities and materials to make art and have their art noticed.

And even in contemporary times it seems that much of the art work on display is of nude women. This reduces women to the role of desirable sexual objects. It makes it more difficult for women to be artists in their own right.

TOP TEN SIGNS THAT YOU'RE AN ART WORLD TOKEN:

10. Your busiest months are February (Black History Month,) March (Women's History,) April (Asian-American Awareness,) June (Stonewall Anniversary) and September (Latino Heritage).

9. At openings and parties, the only other people of color are serving drinks.

8. Everyone knows your race, gender and sexual preference even when they don't know your work.

7. A museum that won't show your work gives you a prominent place in its lecture series.

6. Your last show got a lot of publicity, but no cash.

5. You're a finalist for a non-tenure-track teaching position at every art school on the east coast.

4. No collector ever buys more than one of your pieces.

3. Whenever you open your mouth, it's assumed that you speak for "your people," not just yourself.

2. People are always telling you their interracial and gay sexual fantasies.

1. A curator who never gave you the time of day before calls you right after a Guerrilla Girls demonstration.

A PUBLIC SERVICE MESSAGE FROM **GUERRILLA GIRLS** CONSCIENCE OF THE ARTWORLD
532 LaGUARDIA PLACE, #237 · NY, NY 10012

short credit needed

More women have the opportunity to become artists today. However there still remains a deficit of highly acclaimed women artists compared to men.

Why is this? As one guerrilla girl points out: After doing research 'we found that it was worse than we thought: the most influential galleries and museums exhibited almost no women artists. When we showed the research around, some said it was an issue of quality, not prejudice. Others admitted there was discrimination, but considered the situation hopeless. Everyone in positions of power - curators, critics, collectors, the artists themselves, passed the buck. The artists blamed the dealers, the dealers blamed the collectors, the collectors blamed the critics, and so on.' www.guerrillagirls.com

And largely speaking who were these people in positions of power?........ Men.

In the late 1990's and early 21st century some women artists did make the headlines and gained fame. But more often than not this was because they broke away from the 'norm', and their fame was in part as a result of scorning them for this 'misbehaviour'.

One of the most famous of these was Tracey Emin. In two pieces of work in particular: *Everyone I Have Ever Slept With* and *My Bed*.

Everyone I Have Ever Slept With 1963–1995 was a tent appliquéd with 102 names of the people she had slept with up to the time of its creation in 1995. The title is often misinterpreted as referring to all of Emin's sexual partners, but it includes all the people she ever slept next to as well.

Emin's art subverts the connections between women and craft, while playing on stereotypes about women as sexual objects. The work *My Bed* (1998) was exhibited at the Tate Gallery in 1999. It was shortlisted for the Turner Prize. It consisted of Emin's unmade bed whose ruffled sheets and littered objects conveyed depravity. It gained much media attention. Although it did not win the prize, its notoriety has persisted.

And as highlighted, *My Bed* did not win the Turner Prize. Was Emin being reduced to the status of an art world token as illustrated by the Guerrilla Girls (p.165)?

But fear not, there are some wonderful women who are quite amazing and exciting artists. They can inspire you and show us all how women have achieved fame and respect in the art world.

Whose resilience inspires us?

> Louise Bourgeois
> 25 December 1911 –
> 31 May 2010

Louise Bourgeois had a long and illustrious artistic career. It spanned practically all her life and she continued to create right up to her death at the grand age of 98.

Louise began studying Mathematics and Geometry. After her mother's death in 1932, she abandoned these studies and turned her attention to art. Her tutors noticed her aptitude for sculpture, a medium she used to great effect in her career.

Louise was born in Paris, France, but moved to the United States of America in the 1940s with her husband. At this time she had two sons, developed her talents, and met other artists. Often she was the only woman within artists' groups and Louise is famous for 'making it in a man's world.'

She used the troubling things that happened to her in childhood as a source of inspiration to make incredible art that always made an impact on the people who saw it.

Louise Bourgeois worked across mediums, as she was a very versatile and talented artist. She drew, painted, wrote and stitched. It is for sculpture that she is best remembered. Her most famous work is of a giant spider that she called *Mamman* (Mother), a tribute to her own mother and women's creative power.

Internationally reknowned French Artist

Her work has been, and continues to be exhibited in major art galleries around the world.

Illustration by Harriet Gibson

More, more, more...!

This list of wonderful women artists we hope will invigorate and inspire you:

- Frida Kahlo, a painter from Mexico (1907-1954)
- Mona Hatoum, an installation artist from the Palestinian Territories (1952-)
- Georgia O'Keeffe, an American painter (1887-1986)
- Sarah Lucas, a sculptor, installation artist, and photographer from England (1962-)
- Dame Barbara Hepworth, an English sculptor (1903-1975)
- Annie Leibovitz, an American photographer (1949-)
- Cindy Sherman, a photographer and filmmaker from America (1954-)
- Rachel Whiteread, a sculptor from England (1963-)
- Gillian Wearing, a photographer from England (1963 -)
- Barbara Kruger, an American conceptual artist (1945 -)
- Emma Lonsdale, English painter and textile artist
- Pollie Uttley, English potter (ceramics)
- Sam Tate, English artist and Amnesty International campaigner

 Activity

Find out on the internet or at a library about some of the women above. Pick one that inspires you and create a piece of art in response to their work:

Art isn't just about visual art of course, so here are some other artists to inspire you

Poets

By Ali Hanbury, Viv Whitaker and Lucy Wright

Caroline Bird, Carol Ann Duffy (first female Poet Laureate of course) and Jackie Kay.

Musicians

Amanda Palmer, Patti Smith, Tracey Chapman, Dido, Adele, Nina Simone, Ani difranco, Dar Williams, Emmy the Great, The Be Good Tanyas, Sister Rosetta Tharpe, Annabelle Chvostek, Joni Mitchell, Carole King.

Illustration by Omena Osivwemu

Authors

Toni Morrison, Jeanette Winterson, Dorothy Koomson and Rosie Thomas - all of these fiction writers write about strong women and issues which make 'you' think!
Caitlin Moran (her book is modern, feminist and hilarious).
Val Carpenter & Kerry Young – for everything they wrote about working with girls & young women.
Bea Campbell – for everything she writes about 'society'!
Jacky Fleming, cartoonist - for making us laugh. Eve Ensler - for writing *Vagina Monologues*, We think every girl/young woman should have the opportunity to see this.

Jackie Fleming's book

Whose resilience inspires us?

Sister Rosetta Tharpe
20 March 1915 –
9 October 1973

Pioneering Gospel Singer and God-mother of Rock and Roll

Sister Rosetta was born Arkansas. Her parents were cotton pickers. She started performing when she was four years old. She was described as the 'singing and guitar playing miracle'. Her early life was spent on the road in the Southern states of the USA, with her mother who was a travelling Evangelist. During this time Rosetta became exposed to both Jazz and Blues music.

In the late 1920s the family moved to Chicago. Rosetta continued playing music: Gospel music in public, Jazz and Blues in private. She developed a unique style that mixed these sacred and secular styles, resulting in unforgettable performances.

In 1938 she recorded music for the first time, signing a record deal with Decca Records. Her music caused quite a stir with Churchgoers who were shocked by the way she used Gospel music in 'not-so-holy' ways.

Rosetta continued to record during the Second World War. She recorded the song 'Strange Things Happen Every Day' which has been credited as the first ever Rock and Roll record. After the War she worked with Marie Knight recording the popular song 'Up Above My Head.' With Marie she toured the country and it is rumoured that the pair were lovers.

In the 1950-60s she came to Europe to perform.

Sister Rosetta died of a stroke in 1973. It is only recently that her talent and influence are being celebrated.

Illustration by Harriet Gibson

Whose resilience inspires us?

Evelyn Glennie
19 July 1965

Evelyn was born and raised in Aberdeenshire, Scotland. Her father was an accordionist in a Scottish country-dance band. The strong, indigenous musical traditions of North East Scotland were important in the development of the young musician. She studied at Ellon Academy and the Royal Academy of Music, and was also a member of the National Youth Orchestra of Scotland.

Evelyn was the first full-time solo percussionist in 20th-century western society. She has performed all over the world and has won numerous awards including 'Best Studio and Live Percussionist' from Rhythm Magazine in 1998, 2000, 2002, 2003 and 2004; 'Walpole Medal of Excellence' 2002 and 'Sabian Lifetime Achievement' Award 2006. She was inducted into the Percussive Arts Society's Hall of Fame in 2008.

She has recorded various albums including *Rhythm Song* (1990) and *The Sugar Factory* (2007). She has collaborated with artists such as Björk and appeared on the TV programme 'Sesame Street'.

Evelyn's achievements are remarkable because she has been profoundly deaf since age 12. This does not inhibit her ability to perform at the international level. She regularly plays barefoot

Percussionist extraordinaire

during both live performances and studio recordings in order to 'feel' the music better.

Evelyn argues that deafness is largely misunderstood by the public. This is because she has taught herself to hear with parts of her body other than her ears. She also plays the Great Highland Bagpipes and has her own registered tartan.

Illustration by Harriet Gibson

Whose resilience inspires us?

Queen Latifah
18 March 1970

Latifah was born and raised primarily in East Orange, New Jersey. Her parents divorced when she was ten. Her stage name, *Latifah*, meaning 'delicate' and 'very kind' in Arabic, was given to her by her cousin when she was eight. Always a tall girl, the 5'10' Latifah was a power forward on her high school basketball team.

She began her music career beatboxing for the rap group *Ladies Fresh*. She was signed in 1988. Her first single was called *'Wrath of My Madness'* and her first album *All Hail the Queen* was released in 1989, when she was nineteen.

Singer, Rapper and Actress

In 1998, she released her fourth hip-hop album *Order in the Court*. After *Order in the Court*, Latifah shifted primarily to singing in soul music and jazz standards, which she had used sparingly in her previous hip-hop records. In 2007, she released *Trav'lin' Light*. It features guest appearances from lots of famous people including Stevie Wonder and was nominated for a Grammy.

In the 1990s Latifah began to carve out a career for herself as an actress. She starred in TV programmes such as *The Fresh Prince of Bel-Air* and had her own talk show, *The Queen Latifah Show*. Since 2002 Latifah has had more mainstream success such as receiving an Academy Award nomination for her role as Matron 'Mama' Morton in the Oscar-winning musical film *Chicago*.

Queen Latifah remains an inspiring figure for women Hip-Hop artists. She is also a lesbian icon (but has never officially 'come out') and has her own perfume range.

Illustration by Harriet Gibson

Whose resilience inspires us?

Ari Up
17 January 1962 -
20 October 2010

Ari Up was born in Germany. Her mother would later marry John Lydon from the Sex Pistols. Ari spent her teenage years amidst the growing punk scene in London. Her house was often full of musicians, and she learnt guitar skills from The Clash's Joe Strummer.

Living in such a creative environment led to Ari experimenting with music and style. She formed The Slits with Palmolive, Tessa Pollitt and Viv Albertine when she was just 14.

The punk ethos of the time encouraged people to start bands, even if they had no formal music skills. This was particularly liberating for women who were given little opportunity to try out playing and writing music. When they began, The Slits weren't amazing musicians, but with practise they got better. They also dressed in confrontational ways, which made them fun to look at, as well as to listen to.

Ari Up was a massive fan of reggae music, and this influenced the type of music The Slits made. Their album *Cut* (1979). The album cover shows a picture of the Slits naked covered in mud! It is now recognised as one of the greatest albums of all time. The Slits toured the UK with other punk acts, such as The Clash and The Pop Group. They also toured the United States of America on a number of occasions.

Charismatic lead-singer of punk band, The Slits

The Slits split up in 1981 and Ari went to live in Jamaica with her husband and baby. She continued to make music and released a solo album *Dread More Dan Dead* in 2005. She reformed The Slits in 2006 before her premature death from cancer aged 48.

Illustration by Harriet Gibson

Chapter 10 - It's a big world in here

Throughout this book we have tried to weave threads between time and space. We have looked at herstory and women's lives today. We have at times, looked toward to future. We also want to weave threads that join the whole world together. In this chapter we look at how what is international is local, and how we are all connected as women, wherever we live in the world. We believe women from different countries can learn from each other and support each other, to create a better and fairer world. The world isn't 'out there' as something separate to you - it is in here, in your life and experiences, where you live, and in you.

Sustainability and the environment

by Maggie Cole

What is sustainability?

" **Sustainable** development is development that meets the needs of the present without compromising the ability of future generations to meet their own needs "

Our Common Future, Brundtland, 1987

Photo by Jean Spence

We have to ensure that this planet has sufficient resources to meet current and future needs – and we have to remember that this is for a global population that is always growing.

Whatever we do requires that energy, and with global oil reserves dwindling fast we need to turn to technology allows us to use renewable sources of energy such as the wind, sun and water. We have to use that energy wisely, to continually reuse and recycle the resources that have already been taken to build our 'stuff'.

We are asked to 'Reduce, Re-use, Recycle,' but is this enough to enable a sustainable future for ourselves and our children?

Ellen MacArthur, the World Record-breaking yachtswoman, has launched a Foundation with the purpose of inspiring people to 're-think, to re-design and build a positive future'. It builds on the reduce/re-use/recycle idea but shifts the thinking a bit, to help us build a circular life cycle for those things that we need and use.

What would the world look like if we were happy with just enough 'stuff' to keep us healthy and fulfilled? What if we equally shared resources with all those who are struggling for mere survival on our planet?

Kirsty Scneeberger lead the UK youth delegation at the United Nations Climate Change Talks in Spring 2009. At the talks, the targets for change by the year 2050 were being discussed. In a speech she asked the other delegates: 'How old will you be in 2050?' She said that decision makers now must be able to 'look young people in the eyes and guarantee that they will have a liveable planet in the year 2050. ... we will still be here!' She is campaigning at National and International levels.

What can you do to be more sustainable?

- Support renewable energy projects (wind farms, hydro-power etc)
- Ask your MP what they are doing about climate change and renewable energy (www.findyourmp.parliament.uk)
- At Christmas, why not try to set a cap on how much you spend, e.g. agree as family or friends that £10 per person is enough
- Have you heard of 'bin diving'? (It is where you look through supermarket bins for things that have gone out of day that day, and you take them home and use them instead of them going to landfill)
- When you use a computer, print double-sided and in draft and send off your ink cartridges to be recycled
- Recycle paper, plastic, glass bottles etc
- Turn lights off when you don't need them
- Bring your own bag to the supermarket so you don't have to use a new one

Forests, Food and Freedom

By Niamh Moore

Women hugging trees in the Indian Himalayas is one of the striking images of the 1970s and 1980s for environmentalists and ecofeminists across the world. This movement was called Chipko. The word comes from Hindi and is translated as 'to hug', or 'to cling', or 'to stick to' the trees.

Why were they doing this? To stop developers from cutting the trees down.

This movement involved mainly women, because they were especially affected by deforestation.

Cutting down the trees led to a lack of firewood and food for animals. This meant it was difficult for them to provide food for animals, fuel for heat and fuel for cooking food, therefore it was harder to make a living.

How did logging come about?

Commercial forestry companies were able to exploit the forests, while local people were increasingly excluded. It was local people who relied on using the products of the forests as part of their livelihood.

It was easier for companies because of laws from when the British ruled India. One such law was the Indian Forest Act of 1878, which restricted access to local people who needed to use forests. There were many protest songs and chants from the Chipko movement. In one, the forestry company owner says:

" You foolish village women, do you know what these forests bear? Resin, timber, and therefore foreign exchange!

"

The women answer:

" Yes we know. What do the forests bear? Soil, water and pure air. Soil, water and pure air.

"

175

The Chipko Movement inspired many others in different parts of the world to take action to protect the environment. In 1987, Chipko was awarded the Right Livelihood Award, which is known as the alternative Nobel Prize.

Vandana Shiva is an activist who has been important in telling the story of the Chipko movement. In 1986 she wrote a book called *Staying Alive: Women, Ecology and Development*. Shiva uses the word ecofeminism to link feminism and environmentalism, and to insist on the need for a world where neither women nor nature are exploited.

Shiva is also concerned about the impact of western 'development' practices on countries like India. She is critical of the so-called 'Green Revolution' in India, a controversial change in farming practices introduced in the 1960s. Despite the name, the Green Revolution was not about organic or environmentally-friendly farming. It was about the introduction of industrialised agriculture, involving the use of high-yielding seeds, pesticides and fertilisers.

The Green Revolution was supposed to increase the amount of food that could be grown in India, so that there would be enough food for everyone. However, Shiva thought these farming practices were devastating the soil, and hurting the people who were trying to grow food. They had to sell the food they grew to pay for the chemicals they needed. They ended up hungrier and poorer than they had been, and soil was degraded by the use of chemicals.

There were also changes in the crops people grew, from lentils and beans (which were one of the main foods people ate), to wheat which they did not eat so much of. It was grown to be exported to countries like the UK.

Some people also argue that, even though many people In India have enough food to eat, they are still malnourished because the industrially-produced food is not so nutritionally good. They also argue that famine and lack of food is a political issue, not so much caused by natural crop failures or lack of food, but more caused by how the growing, producing and consuming of food is organised.

Shiva has continued to campaign, to write books, and inspire many across the world. She write about issues around forestry, food, and particularly on the impact of western industrial agriculture on global food, how it is produced and consumed. She has campaigned against genetically modified foods, and highlighted the effects of growing these on farmers in India, some of whom have killed themselves when their livelihoods have been destroyed by debt to global seed companies.

Sugar: Bittersweet?

Many foods we are familiar with have long, complicated histories and processes of how they are produced. One of these is sugar.

Sugar is not only responsible for many health problems for those who eat it, but is also a central part of the long histories of colonialism and slavery.

Much sugar has been grown in countries such as Barbados, Jamaica and other Caribbean Islands, as well as parts of South America. It was grown on plantations, where white industrialists from Britain and other countries bought people from Africa on 'slave ships', and kept people like prisoners, forcing them to work long hours, and punishing slaves brutally when they tried to rebel against being treated in this way. Many women slaves faced the additional brutality of being raped by the white plantation owners. Slavery was officially abolished in most of the British Empire with the Slavery Abolition Act in 1833, but unofficially it continued long after that.

Many other foods and everyday items that we easily take for granted as part of our daily lives have long and brutal histories.

Flowers, for example, are sometimes grown on intensive farms in Africa and Latin America, where workers' health has been ruined by the use of pesticides. Workers have had to work long shifts and in some cases, children labour long and hard picking and packing flowers.

Why food, flowers and clothing are big issues for women

The flower industry and the textile/clothing industry have many more women working in them than men, and many more women in lower paid jobs than men, so these issues are very important for women.

June Hartley, of Women Working Worldwide, a campaigning group for fair rights for women, described the factory she used to work at in South Africa:

> A lot of the women were sexually harassed and ended up in relationships with male co-workers and supervisors. They knew if they didn't, at the very least they wouldn't get the help they often needed in carrying rolls of blankets and fixing broken belts on their weaving machines. At worst, the supervisors would victimise them, for example by refusing to allow them to leave work for family emergencies, or even dismissing them

June was arrested for bringing workers together to form a Union to fight for their rights. She was held in solitary confinement in prison for nearly a year.

She says that she thinks things are getting better, with more awareness of Fairtrade and more ethically minded consumers. There is still a long way for supermarkets to go however, who often stock the cheapest goods instead of those that have been made fairly.

In Tanzania I have seen some positive things, such as a pregnant women working on a farm being given a space to go and rest in. That's definitely new. I also noticed that when the pesticides were sprayed in the fields, the workers were sent away so they wouldn't get contaminated and ill from the sprays. It's key that we get retailers to understand that their buying practices can help regulate factories so their workers don't work too many hours, and so they will pay their workers enough money to live on

June hartley. Women Working Worldwide

Activity

Go and look in your fridge and pick 6 food or drink items. Find out where the food or drink comes from, then look in a book or on the internet to see how women are treated in the countries that have made your food.

Item	Where does it come from?	How women are treated in that country

Cont...

Cont...

Item	Where does it come from?	How women are treated in that country

Do you know what fairtrade means?

If you see the fairtrade label on your food, drinks, clothes or household objects, then it means that the people who have made those things have been give proper wages and fair treatment at work.

Whose resilience inspires us?

Rachel Carson
27 May 1907 –
14 April 1964

Rachel Carson grew up on a small farm in Springdale, Pennsylvania. She was an avid reader and began writing stories at a young age. She was fascinated by nature, in particular the sea.

Rachel studied Biology and Zoology at University, but she was forced into employment to support her family who were facing financial difficulties. Here she began her career as a biologist, working in the U.S. Bureau of Fisheries. She became a full-time nature writer in the 1950s.

Her 1951 book *The Sea Around Us* was a bestseller. It won her financial security and recognition as a gifted writer. Her next book, *The Edge of the Sea*, and the republished version of her first book, *Under the Sea Wind*, were also read widely. Together these books explore the whole of ocean life, from the shores and surface to the deep sea.

In the late 1950s, Carson became interested in conservation and environmental issues, especially the problems caused by synthetic pesticides. The result was *Silent Spring* (1962). The book brought environmental concerns to the attention of the American public. It was massively influential in changing government policy relating to the use of pesticides. It also inspired grassroots environmental movements

Biologist and Conservationaist whose writings inspired the Enviromental Movement

across the world to challenge the ways humans were ruining the planet in the name of scientific 'progress.'

Illustration by Harriet Gibson

181

Whose resilience inspires us?

Wangari Muta Maathai
1 April 1940

Wangari was born in the village of Ihithe in the central highlands of British-controlled Kenya on April 1, 1940. Her family was of the Kikuyu ethnic group, and had lived in the area for several generations.

Wangari did well at school and won a scholarship to study in the United States of America in 1960 where she studied Biology, Chemistry and German. She later studied in Germany. In 1971 she became the first Eastern African woman to receive a Ph.D., when she was granted a Doctorate of Anatomy from the University College of Nairobi.

Wangari became involved in a number of civic organisations in the early 1970s including the Kenya Red Cross Society, the Kenya Association of University Women and worked with The Environment Liaison Centre. Through this work it became evident to Wangari that the root of most of Kenya's problems was environmental degradation.

Wangari is most well known for founding the Green Belt Movement in 1977. The movement encouraged the women of Kenya to plant tree nurseries throughout the country. In 1986 the movement expanded throughout Africa and led to the foundation of the Pan-African Green Belt Network. In the late '80s and '90s the Kenyan government tried

Enviromental and Political Activist, Founder of the Greenbelt Movement

to undermine the Green Belt Movement because of the way it challenged their power. Wangari then became involved in prodemocracy struggles in Kenya.

In 2003 she founded the Mazingira Green Party of Kenya. In 2004 Wangari was awarded the Nobel Peace Prize. She continues to work as an environmental and women's rights activist today.

Illustration by Harriet Gibson

The Girl's Work Resource Unit and International Work

Lancashire Girls Work Resource Unit Poster about their International Work. From Kate Clements and held at the Feminist Webs Archive

Item from Feminist Web Archive

The Soroptimists

Soroptimist International is world-wide service organisation for women. They are committed to a world where women and girls together achieve their individual and collective potential, realise aspirations and have an equal voice in creating strong, peaceful communities worldwide.

Soroptimists inspire action and create opportunities to transform the lives of women and girls through a global network of members and international partnerships. Many Soroptimists fundraise to support women's causes, and have real influence with governments to improve women's lives.

They are very passionate about educating women all over the world. They say:

> If you want to feed someone for a day, you give them a fish; but if you want to feed someone for a lifetime, you educate a woman

Why not find out where your local Soroptimist group is and join them or donate money to one of their causes?

Chapter 11 - Commonality and Difference

by Janet Batsleer

When women get together they can find many things in common about their experiences, even when they come from different classes, different cultural histories or different parts of the world. Often women find this refreshing because they understand each other in ways not understood by men.

But they can also find much difference. Some women are more privileged than others, and some are more disadvantaged. This can lead to unhealthy power dynamics that recreate the oppression of mainstream society. Some women find they have more similarity with men than women, as this participant at the first feminist webs event describes:

When I first heard about feminism in the 1970s, I thought, 'what's all this about posh women getting together and talking about THEIR lives?' I don't live the same life as them. I have more in common with my brother, because we are both working class

June hartley, Women Working Worldwide

Thinking about ways we are similar or different can be a very fruitful source of questioning, learning through experience (experiential learning) and education. It can also strengthen political movements. However these conversations are not easy. They require honesty and understanding. They sometimes create feelings of guilt and painful arguments. This means that political women's groups can often be challenging.

It is important for all people who want to help make a positive change in their world (including you!) to remember that there will be hard times, including times of disagreement. So it is important to look after yourself. Take time for yourself, know when to put all your energies into discussions, and know when to take a step back. Self-care, positive role models and mentors, and not feeling that you need to do everything all-in-one go all help activists enormously to do good work year after year.

It is easy to understand too though, why some people would rather not go out of their own comfort zones and places of safety.

For example (thinking back to the abortion debate in Chapter 3), when women in the UK in the 1970s formed the Women's Abortion Campaign there was an emphasis on the right to abortion. The campaign also emphasised the importance of women, rather than medical professionals, having the right to control the decision about terminating a pregnancy.

However, some disabled people's groups pointed out that in valuing women's choices, the campaign materials sometimes demeaned and devalued the life and existence of disabled people. They pointed out that the example of 'the risk of giving birth to a disabled child' was often used as a reason why people should have an abortion.

Other groups - especially South Asian Women - pointed out that they were positively **encouraged** to terminate pregnancies!

These debates led to a new and stronger focus for campaigning away from just abortion and to the debate about women's control of their own fertility. The Women's Abortion Campaign became the Women's Reproductive Rights Campaign.

In the 1970s and 1980s there were many debates among women and women's groups. Some feminist groups decided to become separate from a wider movement because they wanted to assert their own identity e.g. lesbian feminists and black feminists/ womanists. By the 1990s this fragmentation had changed the face of Feminism, which was both more diverse and less concentrated. This diversity had many positive elements as it helped women who had felt sidelined to have their identity recognised and even celebrated.

The downside however, was that having lots of splinter groups (rather than a single movement) made it hard to have a strong 'single voice' for political change, instead there are hundreds of voices all talking at the same time.

So we should remember our differences, but we should also know when to come together to join our voices collectively to make big changes happen.

Resilience to multiple oppression

the three m's: marriage, motherhood and monotony

When I was nineteen I got pregnant and married to an East London man. He went to university. My life was the two rooms of his parents house we lived in, my son, and the jobs I did to support us. I left home at 7.30 each morning, getting back twelve hours later. The nursery was some distance from the house. Then there was the baby, cooking etc. When I was 24/5 we went to Leeds, when my husband left college. I became 'ill': nervous, withdrawn, isolated, tearful, I hated going out and was always thinking there was something wrong with me. After only a year (it was meant to be at least three) we came back to London. It took months to find somewhere to live, move in etc. The flat we (he) bought was in a middle class part of Lewisham. Then it started again, my withdrawal. I talked constantly about the middle class people I was living amongst, how I couldn't/wouldn't fit in, but it was a long time before I began to connect my withdrawal with that pressure—to adapt to the middle classes.

Extract from Trouble and Strife magazine in the Feminist Webs Archive

THE SIX DEMANDS

1. Admit you're middle class

2. Admit we're working class

3. Stop thinking you're better than us
   (Who's hostile?)

4. Stop trying to control our access to the Women's
   Liberation Movement:
   > practically
   > verbally
   > emotionally

5. Shar your education skills, connections, property, money
   with us

6. Confront classism whenever you see it, in yourself and in
   other women. Be prepared to break rank

THE SIX DEMANDS

*AND NOW FOR SOMETHING
COMPLETELY DIFFERENT.................build a working
class women's movement.............build a working class
women's movement...............build a working class
women's movement............................*

I'M A WORKING CLASS WOMAN OK?

WE'RE WORKING CLASS WOMEN OK!

Extract from Trouble and Strife magazine in the Feminist Webs Archive

We need to understand how being pushed down in society - oppressed - can affect not just women, but lots of groups. So imagine you belong to a number of these groups, for example, you are a black, disabled woman who is a lesbian. You face lots of discrimination from lots of places, and you might find that very few places accept you for all that you are.

As a disabled bisexual, in a disabled space my sexuality was ignored. When I went to the Lesbian and Gay Group, it was hard enough to fight for bisexual rights, let alone have disability issues recognised too. Nowhere and no-one saw me for everything I am

Participant at feminist webs event, 2006

Activity

Find out a bit about these women or groups:

- The Black Womanism Movement
- Olive Morris and the Black Panthers
- Organisation of Women of Asian and African Descent (OWAAD)
- The Lesbian Avengers
- Sisters Against Disableism (S.A.D)

What other groups can you find for women with disabilities, women of different races and religions, women of different classes, older women, younger women, women with children?

Disbility right poster in the Feminist Webs Archive

Whose resilience inspires us?

How have these women and groups helped women build resilience? Here are some Spirit Women that we think help embody some of the ideas of commonality and difference, and were just too darn exciting to not put in this book!

Octavia E.Butler
22 June 1947 –
24 February 2006

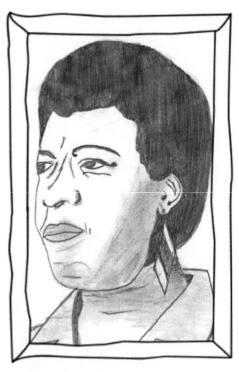

Octavia was born and raised in Pasadena, California. She grew up in a struggling, racially mixed neighborhood. As a child she was a daydreamer and shy, and was later diagnosed as being dyslexic. She began writing at the age of 10 'to escape loneliness and boredom.'

Her interest in Science Fiction began when she was 12. In her late teens she took writing classes where she developed her skills. She remained, throughout her career, a self-identified science fiction fan, an insider who rose from within the ranks of the field.

Her first published story, *Crossover*, appeared in a 1971 Sci-Fi anthology. Her first book *Patternmaster* was published in 1976. This became a series of five stories. In 1979 she published *Kindred*, a novel that uses the science-fiction concept of time travel to explore slavery in the United States. It has remained one of her most widely read novels.

Octavia Butler was a prolific writer. She wrote many novels and short stories. She used the genre of Science Fiction to explore modern and ancient social issues, particularly relating to

Science Fiction Writer

race, sexuality, gender, religion, social progress and class.

She won many awards including the Nebula Award for Best Science Fiction Novel for *Parable of the Talents* in 1999. In 2010, four years after her death, she was inducted into the Science Fiction Hall of Fame, a museum based in Seattle in the United States of America.

Illustration by Harriet Gibson

Whose resilience inspires us?

Mary Seacole
1805 - 14 May 1881

Mary Seacole was born Mary Jane Grant in Kingston, Jamaica. She was the daughter of a white Scottish officer in the British Army and a free Jamaican Creole woman. Seacole was proud of her Scottish ancestry and called herself a Creole.

Seacole's mother was a 'doctress', a healer who used traditional Caribbean and African herbal remedies. She ran a boarding house in Kingston. Many of the residents were disabled European soldiers and sailors, often suffering from the epidemic yellow fever. Here Mary acquired her nursing skills.

In her twenties she worked alongside her mother as a nurse. Occasionally she was called to assist at the British Army hospital. Nursing enabled her to travel across the Caribbean, journeys which she kept a record of in her journal. For a woman of that time, her independent spirit and her preference to travel without a male chaperone was rare.

In 1836 she married Edwin Horatio Hamilton Seacole in Kingston. It was claimed that he was the illegitimate son of Admiral Nelson, the British naval captain. He would die in 1844 leaving Mary widowed.

Mary is perhaps best known for 'nursing work' in the Crimean War

Inspirational Nurse, Healer, Writer and Traveller

(October 1853 - 1 April 1856). Some modern historians even say she was the first (unofficial) female doctor rather than a nurse.

The Crimean War was fought between the Russian Empire and an alliance of the United Kingdom, France, the Kingdom of Sardinia, and the Ottoman Empire. Due to the large numbers of soldiers in one place, cholera broke out. Mary's skill and experience in dealing with the disease meant she saved many soldiers' lives. The British army called her 'Mother Seacole.'

Illustration by Harriet Gibson

After the war Seacole published a 200-page autobiographical account of her travels, *Wonderful Adventures of Mrs. Seacole in Many Lands*. It was the first autobiography written by a black woman in Britain.

After her death, Mary's life faded from public memory. Florence Nightingale, a white woman who also served in the Crimean War, was often remembered instead of Mary. Things have now improved and in 2004, Mary was voted to be the greatest Black Briton of all time.

Understanding Gender

Some of the ways we feel commonality and some of the difficulties we face with our differences, are related to the way we understand and interpret gender.

This activity below helps unpick some of the ways that we understand our own gender, and other people's gender.

Gender identity

Male   Gender Neutral/   Female
             Gender Variant/
             Gender 'Queer' *

This is about how we inwardly feel about our gender, how we think about our own gender

(*remember the word queer should be used with caution)

Gender Expression

Feminine   Androgynous   Masculine

This is about how we want to express our gender e.g. the way we act, dress, talk, walk, hobbies etc. This is separate to gender identity

Biological Sex

Vagina, Ovaries, Womb   Intersex   Penis, Testicles

This is about what biology we have and includes chromosomes. There are many combinations of sex chromosomes e.g. XX, XY, XXY, XYY etc. Many babies are born intersex, and in the past doctors would 'correct' intersex or indeterminate sexual organs, e.g. to create a vagina. This has causes distress to people who, as they grow older, do not feel that they 'fit' with the sex that the doctor assigned them.

Sexual Orientation

Heterosexual ('straight')   Bisexual/   Lesbian or Gay
                                  Pansexual/
                                  Asexual

This is about 'who we fancy', including our emotional and physical attraction to someone else, or whether we feel sexual attraction at all.

Activity

Think about, and perhaps plot on the lines above, where you think you are. Perhaps you can be in more than one place on a line, or over time where you place yourself changes?

Trans women are women who feel their gender identity does not match their biological sex.

It has sometimes been difficult for trans women and for gender-non-conforming women to be accepted in women-only space. This has been debated about since the late 1970s. There is no consensus on transgender issues amongst all feminists. Issues of gender and sexuality are complex, overlapping and sometimes contradictory, but trans people have contributed much to the ways we can and will all understand gender diversity.

Kate Bornstein
15 March 1948

Kate was born in Neptune City, New Jersey and was assigned a male sex at birth. She studied Theater Arts at Brown University, graduating in 1969. In the 1970s Kate was a member of the Church of Scientology. She became disillusioned with the movement and left it in 1981.

Kate is transgender but was never comfortable with the belief that all trans women are 'women trapped in men's bodies'. Bornstein did not identify as a man, but the only other gender option was to be a woman. As there were no other routes to go down, she had gender reassignment surgery in 1986.

Since this time she has made performances, delivered lectures, facilitated workshops and written books that are critical of how society organizes people in terms of a 'gender binary'. That means we divide everything up into two opposites of male and female, rather than seeing gender as something fluid or continuous.

Kate proclaims herself a 'gender outlaw'.

Like many other people in the world, her gender is neither male nor female. It is something else. Kate still uses the pronoun 'she,', but sometimes she uses 'hir' or 'ze.' Kate is the author of many wonderful books that explore gender and identity in funny and tender ways. These include *Gender Outlaw: On Men,*

Writer, Performance Artist, Gender Outlaw

Women, and the Rest of Us (1994), *My Gender Workbook: How to Become a Real Man, a Real Woman, the Real You, or Something Else Entirely* (1997) and *Hello Cruel World: 101 Alternatives to Suicide for Teens, Freaks and Other Outlaws* (2006).

In *Hello Cruel World* she offers the following advice:

'You do anything it takes—anything at all—to make your life more worth living. There's only one rule that makes that sort of blanket permission work: Don't be mean. That's the only rule you ever need to follow to make sure that your life is gonna get better.'

Illustration by Harriet Gibson

Thinking about race differences - Omena and her mum's writing

by Omena and Kimberley Osivwemu

Omena - At the same time I got involved with Feminist webs and we discussed image and how to make girls image of themselves more positive, I went to street dance classes, and felt I fitted in, as we were all brown girls with curly or afro hair of all different sizes and shades of brown skin. Around this time I was introduced to the magazine *Black Beauty and hair*, and my mum took me and my sisters to the *Black Beauty and Hair* show in London.

This was the first time I remember seeing so many black people in one place that wasn't Nigeria. I was fascinated, with all the crazy hair colours and styles. I began to realise natural afro hair can be beautiful, and that I can be beautiful naturally. This idea didn't stick though!

I used to wish I had blonde hair and blue eyes, and that my hair would go ,swish swish' when I moved my head from side to side. It made my Mum laugh. I thought she was really cruel, she laughed raucously out loud. I thought she was poorly, that her heart had stopped or something, but she was laughing, she said it was about 'being an outsider'. When she said 'being an outsider' I thought she meant we were living in a tent when everyone else was living in houses.

'No. No.' she said 'its not that! Its how we are- we're treated as outsiders, as if we don't belong.' I asked her what she meant and she explained, telling us a story about when she was younger. Lots of black girls put the school cardi's on their heads with the sleeves hanging down and then swung their heads around. So their cardi' hair went ,swish swish'. She laughed and laughed remembering this and thinking about the swish swish of my imaginary hair.

'But I was different you see,' she wheezed, 'because I have what was called growing hair! '

I was very confused now- what did she mean? Cardigan hair, floppy hair, growing hair. I wanted better explanations!

'Well my hair grows !' My mum wheezed on, 'on my legs, my chins, my head my body- everywhere! I've got growing hair. '

I was left baffled. My mums' hilarity had left me confused.

'But didn't you dye your hair mum?' I quizzed her.

'Yes of course love,' she grinned again, 'I had purple stripes in my head and a beautiful blue and purple tracksuit to match it. I loved it.'

That wasn't what I meant. I wondered if mum was being deliberately evasive and wouldn't take my moans seriously. I wanted long, blonde swishy hair. Like Barbie or even Bratz dolls. Again mum looked at me grinning.

'I remember Barbie, we had loads of

Barbies, but Sylvie cut all their hair off AND their faces out and moved them around. Like that film- was it Toy Story- where the bad boy destroyed the toys, mixing them up to make different toys.'

Mum just didn't take my complaints about my hair seriously at all, did she! She would not listen.

My hair was very very curly, I remember when I was three; I had so much hair I thought it was bigger than my birthday cake! I thought if I held up my birthday cake my hair would still show around the sides of it. It was sooo big and curly, but it also hung down. So maybe that was what Mum meant by "growing hair".

There was a massive life size doll that we had in nursery with blue eyes, pink skin, blond hair. I would fight everyone to play with as I loved her. However,

at home all my dolls were brown, my favourite being a little bald, brown cloth doll called Gracie. But I abused Gracie: chewing and burning her fingers in the fire place!

At school I had many more small friends with long hair and blue or green eyes, and that's what I decided I should look like, and I guess this idea still lingers now.

Not only did I feel I would be more acceptable if I were like them, but I would also fit in better, and people would not have to make exceptions for me as they did in nursery in the play Goldilocks.

Traditionally, Goldilocks is called that because she has golden hair, although – it seemed to me, it wasn't significant to the story. So, when I was made to be „Curly locks" in the Goldilocks play at nursery I was outraged! We have a photo of me at about the age of three or four, screwing my face up, dressed in a frilly pink dress sat on a stage next to three little boys with bear masks. That was our Curly-locks play!

Why I had to be Curly-locks when Goldilocks had curly hair anyway was beyond me! The three little pink skinned boys with bear masks weren't painted brown; so why couldn't I have a gold wig to match my pink frilly (disgusting) frock! All the Disney princesses wore pink dresses; they were all pink skinned. The first brown Disney Princess Tiana in the Princess and the Frog wears green and blue frocks. Not pink! Although I could not say this as I was a toddler, I did run off the stage and refused to participate in any of it!

Lancashire poster

I wanted to be Goldilocks, so why did they have to change the name for me? Why single me out and highlight that I was different? The hair was not really an issue in the story, so why make it an issue for me?

I suppose they were being nice, trying to accommodate me. You know when people are too nice to you because you look different, when you just want to be treated the same as everyone else.

It is not exactly racist but it shows that they don't think they should treat you like everyone else - because you are brown.

'I don't see why they did not stick me as one of the bears, they are brown anyway! ' I retorted back at mum, as she swung around the kitchen, winding her waist with her arms in the air singing, 'Curly locks, do do do do- do', swinging her cardi hair around in the air like Medusa and her snakes.

I've always felt as though I'm different from those around me, and the Curly-locks episode sticks out for me in my childhood.

Amongst some people like my Dad's

Nigerian family I'm light, so I am treated more like a guest. Amongst others, like my Mum's family I'm dark, although we are all multiple heritage.

In primary school and high school until year 9 (third year) I was classed as one of the biggest, and therefore aggressive. There were other brown girls in primary school, but we all seemed to be different from one another, there were a lot who were Caribbean; unlike my best friends at the time who all had long ‚floppy' hair and were thin and pink.

It was only as I began to explore how I saw myself, not how others viewed me that I felt most comfortable and like I fitted in. This happened around the age of 14 -15. In high school I had a group of friends that were all brown, mostly Nigerians and a Jamaican girl, we had a great time together, until I decided I wanted to mix with people of all different backgrounds.

My best friends for a while were, a petite Nigerian girl Mitarie and a short pretty Jamaican girl Tasha, we did everything together and simply accepted each others differences. Me and Tasha even bought the same dresses and earrings, and would go about town being giggly teenage girls!

I also felt like I belonged in my carnival dance troupe too, but that is a whole other story to tell!

Lancashire poster

Lancashire poster

Sexuality

Difference can be a source of joy or a source of pain. A group of young lesbian and bisexual young women in Manchester created the following cartoon which explores sexuality and difference.

My name's Ella, I'm seventeen years old and I'd been feeling utterly depressed. Not just feeling a little bit sad, like all my friends and family assumed... I'd been feeling like everything was dark, black and hopeless.

I felt lost and lonely and I sometimes felt like I was never going to get out of that hole. Sometimes I just thought "what's the point?" I didn't feel like it was worth going to college, seeing friends or even just getting out of bed. Sometimes I felt so low I felt like hurting myself.

Illustrations by Hebe Phillips

You might ask what a woman like me has to be depressed about.
I live in a nice house, my parents are still together, I've got great mates, a good education and i'm in a stable relationship.

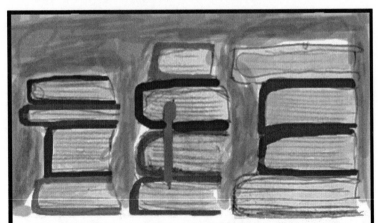

Sounds like the perfect life, right? Well you're wrong. I'd been so stressed with college work. Everyone expects me to be really successful and get a good job and make lots of money...
Although my dad was SO "kind" to let me do art as an A Level and I love it. But it doesn't feel enough.

On top of that, I was having problems in my relationship. I'd been with this amazing woman, Jayne for nearly four months. She's beautiful and amazing and very much out, while I was hiding very much in the closet. It made everything so much more difficult.

It's just so stressful, trying so hard to be somebody I'm not. I was putting this above thing I really cared about. All the work had left me exhausted and tired and I didn't have time to do any time to do anything that made me happy and me.
I'd had enough and I was ready to explode...

We couldn't hold hands or kiss or anything in public. Everything was like some big, dirty, sordid secret hidden behind closed doors. I could tell that it was really starting to bother her, and I started to worry about losing her to some better, more out lesbian.

A few months later...

I thought for a long time about whether I should take pills, but I decided not to. They're not for everyone. I signed up to see a counsellor at 42nd Street and they talked me through some amazing ways to make myself feel better without having to take anti-depressants or hurting myself.

My name's Ella, and I'm still seventeen years old; I'd been feeling utterly depressed, but not anymore. I'd tried everything to make myself feel better, and now I do!

So now, when I feel down, I know loads of things I can do to get myself feeling OK again. I can take a bath, or eat some chocolate, or write in my diary or a poem. Sometimes I'll listen to music. Other times I'll read a book and let my mind escape me away to another place; maybe even a different world.

Best of all though, the thing that always makes me feel better is drawing... or painting... or sculpting... anything even remotely 'arty'. It's such a release and it always allows me to get my feelings out and definitely makes me feel better!

Illustrations by Hebe Phillips

Age

At Feminist Webs, women of all ages come together to have meetings, run events, make resources and campaign. This brings with it many joys as well as many challenges. How we talk to each other can be really tricky. The older women sometimes use language that seems old fashioned or that younger women don't understand. In turn, the younger women use lots of modern words and slang that is lost on the older women. The women who are neither old or young sometimes act as translators in between. What we all have to do is be patient with each other, to try to talk to each other either in simple terms or in words that we explain to people as we go.

In the next chapter we look at youth work and working with young women, but what about older women, what issues and ideas are central to them?

What are the issues as women get older?

By Margaret Beetham

'Older than what?' is the question. At 15, we think 25 is old, at 55 it seems very young. However, our bodies, minds and relationships do change as we get older, so there are issues involved in all three – whatever age we take as a starting point. Feminists have pointed out some of the things which women face as they age.

Because women still routinely take responsibility for caring - whether for children or aging parents - this is often an issue for older women. Motherhood, whenever women enter it, changes the way we live and raises new problems and new joys – as indeed does not having children (if our family, our culture or our peers all think that is how women justify their existence).

Because our culture is so youth-obsessed, particularly in relation to women's appearance, having an aging body, with sagging bits or wrinkles, can be hard for women, especially if we have not come to terms with the tyranny/injustice of being defined by how we look.

Older women are often invisible, and not only on TV, where women news readers get sacked while their male counterparts remain in the limelight. These men wearing their wrinkles and silver hair proudly.

Aging bodies can bring physical problems: aches, pains, failing eyesight or worse. Women live longer than men but are more likely to live in poverty and ill health. Both can be difficulties for us in our old age.

As we grow older, it can be embarrassing to acknowledge that we remain sexual beings. We want to love and be loved – just as, though perhaps differently from - the way we did when young.

The book *Ourselves Growing Older,* the sequel to the famous 1970s feminist text, *Our Bodies Ourselves*, is still a good guide to all this.

But growing older brings new pleasures:

- Long friendships have their own special flavour
- Children growing up, or grown up, and grand-children bring their own delights
- Perhaps as we age we come to know ourselves better, so we no longer have to pretend to be other than who we are
- Being invisible, though hugely annoying, means you can sometimes get away with being deviant

Getting older can be great for women!

Chapter 12 - Young, gifted and girls

When we talk to young women about feminist history and women's history, many times they have said, 'why don't we learn these things in school?' and they are right. We should learn about women's history in schools, and also learn about all the social and political influences that affect our lives as women. But this learning doesn't stop at the school gates. We all joined Feminist Webs because we are passionate about youth work, which includes working with young women outside of schools, for examples in youth clubs, in parks, libraries and community centres. Youth work is a way of working that starts with the knowledge young people have, and the experiences in their own lives, and builds on this. It's a way of thinking that values young people as equal to adults. Feminist youth work unlocks huge amounts of potential, not only from young women, but also from women of all ages who have been involved in it.

Feminist Webs

by Viv Whittaker

As an 'older' feminist having the opportunity to be part of this group has allowed me to be able to mix with young women, and listen to their views about the many issues which affect them (and us).

I have particularly enjoyed the sessions when we all come together to discuss certain topics or work on the archive. The archive has been such a great 'tool' for many workers to use – I'm very proud of it! But of course Feminist Webs is responsible for many other excellent pieces of work too.

Many years ago when I was working in a Youth Service with girls and young women, I used to work hard to keep up to date on the issues affecting them – the many pressure they were under etc… now that I no longer do face-to-face work with young women, it means that I am removed from their experiences.

This was evident when one Saturday morning in a workshop with young women – one of them talked about her sister wanting a pole-dancing kit for Christmas – she was 8 years old!!! And many young women discussed the advantages and disadvantages of mobile phones, as texting is now used to bully and pressure people. None of this was around in my day, and my day was not so long ago! So now I'm involved with this group, I find out what new pressures young women have to face each and every day – as well as having all the old pressures because they haven't gone away!

Feminists Webs is about work with young women – who they are and how they live their lives. It takes the needs of young women seriously – and that's why I'm involved. Thank you for giving me this opportunity.

The History / Herstory of Youth Work with young women and girls

by Jean Spence

There have been two very significant periods in the development of youth work with girls and young women, and these have coincided with key points in feminist activist history.

The first was between the 1870s and 1914, and the second blossomed during the 1970s and early 1980s.

'First wave' feminists wanted full citizenship for women through the suffrage campaign (women getting the right to vote). This happened at the same time as other social activist movements began in the UK, for example working class people's rights.

Through voluntary 'social' work, middle class women extended their domestic skills into the public sphere to help their poorer 'sisters'.

This happened through the growth of existing organisations such as the Young Women's Christian Association (YWCA, est. 1855) and the creation of new Women's Settlements and Girls Clubs. These included organisations such as the Girls' Friendly Society (1874), The Girls' Life Brigade (1902), The Girl Guides (1910) and the National Organisation of Girls Clubs - NOGC (1911). All of these groups responded to the cultural need to carry out girls' work. And why did they do this? It was to help girls organise, learn and find recreational relief from work and domestic drudgery/ boredom. At the same time girls would acquire the qualities associated with 'femininity'.

Single gender organisations were not consciously 'feminist' and sometimes quite the opposite. The groups reflected the wider society at that time. For example, they believed in (and sometimes supported) very separate roles for women and men, and the need to 'protect' female sexual reputations.

Although the club worker Emmeline Pethick Lawrence became a notable suffragette, mostly female youth workers did not think of themselves as political activists. They were inspired by religion rather than politics.

For example, Flora Freeman was an evangelical Christian club worker who set up a Catholic Guide troop. Lily Montagu, who became the first Chairwoman of the National Organisation of Girls Clubs (NOGC), was motivated by her Judaism to address the working conditions of immigrant Jewish girls. Maude Stanley of the Soho Girls' Club who founded the Girls' Club Union was informed by her membership of the Church of England.

The influence of religious youth work declined after the First World War, and so too did single sex female organisations.

The war had challenged gender boundaries established in the Victorian period and after women gained the vote in 1918, they appeared to have achieved their main demand for citizenship status.

Although the YWCA, the GFS and the Guides maintained their single sex focus and organisation, girls' clubs experienced increasing pressure to become mixed. The NOGC responded to the fashion of the times, replacing its focus on industrial reform with questions about 'youth' in general and becoming increasingly mixed gender. The history of the name changes of 'NOGC' is an indicator of the decline of girls' work in the organisation:

- 1911 National Organisation of Girls' Clubs
- 1926 National Councils of Girls' Clubs
- 1944 National Association of Girls' Clubs and Mixed Clubs
- 1953 National Association of Mixed Clubs and Girls' Clubs
- 1961 National Association of Youth Clubs (NAYC)
- 1987 Youth Clubs UK
- 2000 UK Youth

Despite the loss of focus on single-sex girls' work, and its name changes, the NOCG (created for and by women) remained crucial to the continuity of work with girls and young women, in a period of feminist decline. It was key to the establishment of feminist work with girls in the 1970s.

From within the organisation, Pearl Jephcott for instance, continued to champion the specific interests and needs of girls during the 1940s whilst Josephine MacAlister Brew made an enormous contribution to thinking about informal and social education in youth work during the 1940s and 50s.

During her time as General Secretary between 1953 and 1966, Lesley Sewell established the terms of reference for developmental youth work. This helped the NAYC renew its commitment to working with girls during the second wave of feminism.

The appointment of a girls' worker, Val Carpenter, and the establishment of a Girls Work Unit in 1976, helped to sustain and inform a national movement for work with girls that was explicitly feminist. It was determined to address the conditions of young women's lives and the politics of everyday life and relationships, as well as a politics of social action.

This Girls' Work Unit was subsequently closed in 1986, coinciding with the decline of widespread feminist activism and a second decline in single sex youth work. Its legacy remains in the work underway at present to revive an explicitly feminist youth work practice with young women through Feminist Webs.

UK Youth made this mug to commemorate 100 years of girls' work in their organisation that was once called the National Organisation of Girls' Clubs

Examples of youth work with young women today...

Feminist Webs has been working with some groups of young women across the North West, in Stockport, Manchester, Tameside and Halton. We explored the theme 'women and resilience' (being strong). We went away on a residential together, where the different groups met each other, and learnt about resilience by creating a time line together and getting involved in different workshops delivered by older women in Feminist Webs. The groups then action planned and delivered their own events in their local area, to explore the theme of 'Resilience' and to help women gain strength and support. Here are some examples of what they did.

Young, Gifted and Female

By the young women of Brinnington

Eight young women living in the Brinnington area of Stockport wanted to celebrate the inner strengths of women. During a residential in September, the girls planned to deliver an event in their area called **'In Your Face.'**

The young women planning their event

The aims of the day were: to raise awareness of domestic violence, celebrate being a woman and display art-work that the girls had created, which conveyed the message that we all hide behind a mask.

For example, a by having a beautiful image on the outside, but a message on the inside stating, '*I may look like a pretty face but I am dying on the inside*'.

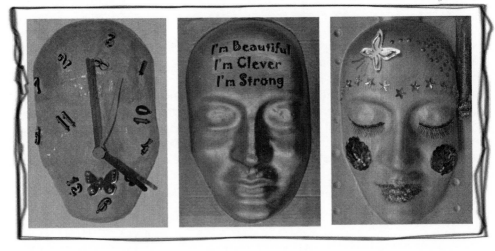

The girls designed forty-eight masks in total that opened up as 3D books with another face (true feeling/image) beneath the mask. The girls also created fifty blank faces for local community members to design.

Some of the designed masks (top) and masks of the blank faces before decorating (above)

The event was informal and fun, offering local community members of all ages, the opportunity to forget their troubles for a little while. People participated in the designing of masks, henna and face painting, free tea, coffee and cakes, a sing-a-long, music and a dance.

Using a youth and community work approach we were able to reach out to almost 400 local community members. The girls' sense of fun, in addition to their energy and enthusiasm, encouraged everyone (young and old alike) to have a go.... And celebrate being a strong woman.

Above left: Young women who organised the event
Above right: A participant showing us her henna art
Left: A display on the day about famous women's resilence

Domestic violence is very complex and frequently hidden. The way in which the Brinnington girls addressed this issue and interacted with the community, was not only innovative but also revolutionary, because their event addressed the issue in a very subtle way. Some of these comments (below) were incorporated into the masks. During the day, some women asked the organisation Stockport Without Abuse for help and support. the organistaion had a low key presence on the day, so people could speak to them without being "seen" speaking to them. Through this the group and the event helped people take the first steps to get out of abusive situations.

Show me you
 me

If I could see myself
would I change?

Don't let him Bring you down

He chooses
my clothes &
things I wear

Trying to hide the pain
but it's still pushing through

He's Watching, He's waiting
Teach your son
How to respect women

Don't judge a book
by its cover

Look inside
What do you see?

Look at yourself
What do you see?

If it was my mate
I would tell her to leave

The Persuader The Liar

sorry, sorry, sorry
sorry, sorry, sorry
but when will it stop?

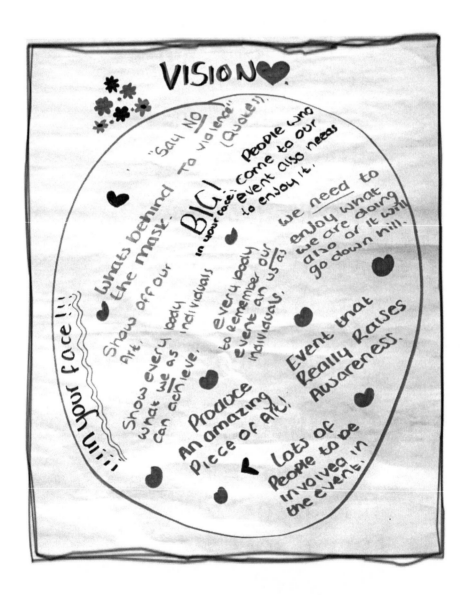

The Brinnington Girl's Vision November 2011

Actual Event: In Your Face, November 2011

The following pages show examples from the project:

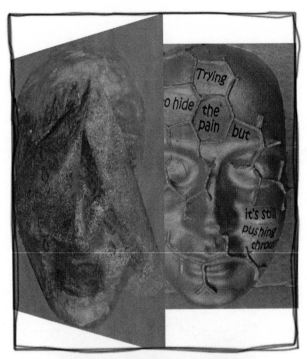

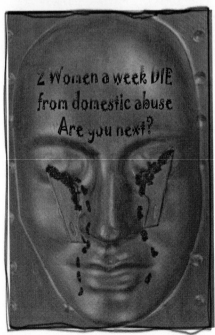

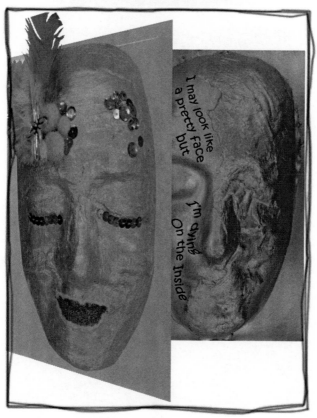

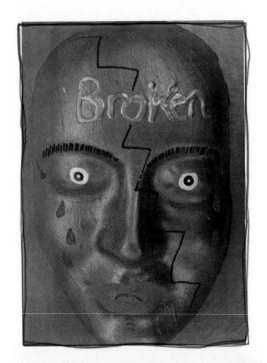

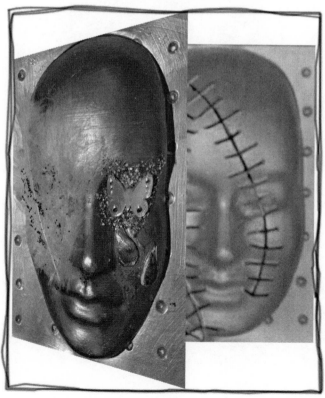

Our Histree

Our piece of work came about from a visit to the Feminist Webs event 'The Carnival of Resilience.' This was a chance for women of all ages to come together and look back throughout history to explore how women have become strong and resilient.

We took part in a range of inspiring activities. We were asked to plan and create our own event and art piece to celebrate women's resilience, including the resilience of women in our local community. We decided for our artwork to create a tree - using leaves made from clay that were inscribed with words that were meaningful, powerful and inspiring to women and described how women were strong.

These were made by local women of all ages from our area and community - including our young women's group, the vicar, councillors and residents.

These leaves were then attached to willow branches. We decided to call our creation: 'Women's Histree.' (see p.224-225 for our leaves)

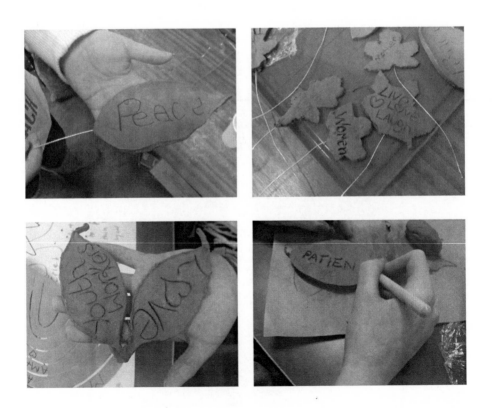

Halton Young Women's views on...

n a preparation workshop the young women discussed and wrote down their thoughts on various projects. we have reproduced these below:

...Body image

- I love my curves but hate that fashion tries to hide them
- Lead by example – as a mum, if you are proud of yourself, your daughter will be proud of themselves too
- So long as you are proud of the person you are, does your image matter?
- Size doesn't matter
- Girls aren't the only sex with insecurities

...Female role models

- Female fire fighters are great because they are proving people wrong
- Beyonce is a role model because she's beautiful and strong
- My mum helps everyone and anyone she can, she will go out of her way, she never gives up when she fails at something
- My grandma – she raised me to be a proud young lady and brought up a great family

...What's important to you?

- My friends and family
- Being myself
- Equality

...The issues affecting young women in today's society

- TV
- Magazines
- Films

The way they put people down for not being 'perfect.'

...Objects that are associated with women

- Make-up
- Dolls
- Bags
- Shoes
- Plastic

...Names for women you don't like

- Easy
- Whore
- Slut
- Plastic bitches
- Baby
- Chick
- Slags
- Bird
- Blond
- Tramp

....What we would like to be known as

- Use my name
- Independent
- Mum

- Grandma
- Unique
- Me

Herstory through History

By Hebe Phillips and the Young Lesbian and Bisexual Women's health Project - LYK:T - in Manchester

History is something we refer to as a way to explore the past and record the present. However, parts of history seem to be sparse in content from women and about women.

We thought about how important HERSTORY is and we decided the life of 'invisible women' was a story that must be told.

'Herstory through History' was an intergenerational event that was open to people of any gender or any sexuality, provided they wanted to find out more about women's history and feminism.

The day was full of discussions, facts and food, and it was lovely to see everyone come together and appreciate the impact women have had in history. The highlight was an incredibly moving story, *The Red Room*, told by Ruthie Boycott Garnet. It was taken from a book of Indian lesbian writing called *Facing the Mirror*, edited by Ashwini Sukthankar.

A relaxing environment allowed everyone to ask questions, and for our young and older women to share their knowledge.

Ruthie the Stroyteller tells a tale of lesbian romance in India

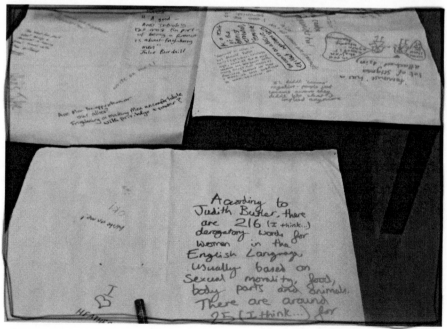

Our quotation table cloths gave people a chance to think about feminism

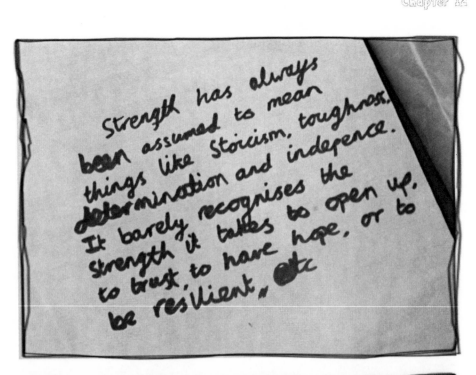

Strength has always been assumed to mean things like Stoicism, toughness, determination and indepence. It barely recognises the strength it takes to open up, to trust, to have hope, or to be resilient, etc

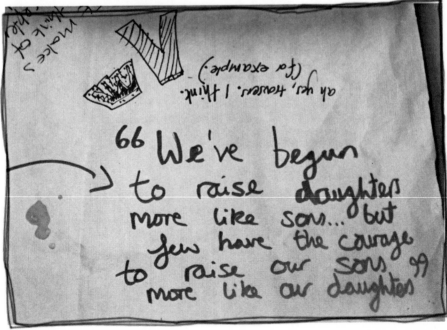

oh yes, flowers, I think. (for example)

66 We've begun to raise daughters more like sons... but few have the courage to raise our sons more like our daughters 99

Quote by Gloria Steinem

My Great Grandmother,
Philis Hodgekins:
At the age of 83, after
raising 2 children, 5
grandchildren and 5 great-
grandchildren, she finished
her life completely
independent, living alone in a
3 storey flat, even when her
stomach was being eaten
away by cancer the only help
she

Taken from the stones that the group worked to create a 3-D wicker heart, with the stones weaved between the branches

The politics of fashion

By St Peters Youth, Ashton

Eyes Wide shut

By SPY Inspire Group

In September 2011 the Inspire Group attended the Girls Are Strong residential and did a lot of work around women's resilience. The group worked alongside girls groups from across the North West.

From this residential the girls were inspired to organize an event of their own for their community to show what they had learnt. From then the group of 15 girls met every week researching more about resilience. Reflecting on their own lives and experiences.

Through the research the girls learned more about the reality of how young women's self image is influenced today – and also had debates and discussions about where these influences are coming from:

- Competition to attract the opposite sex
- Competition to look better than the next person
- To look good
- Not being judged
- To be free
- Magazines
- Media

They concluded that the way you dress effects the way you are treated by society and from their experiences the way they dress is more focussed on (and 'corrected' by) family, peers and society than it is for males. They began to think about how they could dress differently and how that would affect how society treats them. They thought about how females are stereotyped from the style of fashion they choose.

They also discussed other topics relating women such as:

- Breast cancer
- Periods
- Clothes
- Make-up
- Tattoos
- Piercings
- Sports
- Family life
- Playboy bunny merchandise

These affect their everyday lives differently than they do for males. They looked at how females are strong enough to deal with all these extra challenges in life with strength and resilience.

From all of the above, the girls decided to plan their unique Fashion Show 'Eyes Wide Shut'. They chose this name because people in society see what's happening but choose to ignore the truth.

The aim of the event is to firstly give the girls the confidence to dress as they like, and secondly, to provide the opportunity for them to challenge the stereotypes.

To do this, the girls created outfits which they might wear, that would tend to get a negative reaction from others and lead to stereotyping and 'correction'. The audience would express the first reaction that comes into their head. The girls would then respond with the truth - almost myth busting allowing the audience to hear the truth and change their perception of women challenging the idea that you judge on first appearance.

Through this event the girls hope they will become stronger at being who they want to be and be more confident in challenging others who try to correct/change them. It is hoped the audience members will become more open minded and think twice before they judge or correct in future.

The Spy group

So, what are the elements of good work with girls and young women?

Here are some ideas of what makes good feminist youth work.

These were taken from notes from the Girls Work Network Meeting ran by the North West Regional Youth Work Unit convened by Mary Kenny in 2007. The Girls Work Network meets about 4 times a year, for a general catch up about what girls work we are all doing. We plan and run training and conferences for girls workers too. It is also somewhere where we can have important conversations about topical women's issues, and where we get the chance to talk to each other, share ideas, discuss issues and build support.

Good quality youth work with girls and young women is....

- Language – commonality and difference - understanding class
- History – women's politics, Greenham, Pankhurst Centre, women's history – link to globalism, trafficking, national work with Girls' Unit was there once, but not now!
- Challenging the myth that girls work is 'the easy option'
- Not working half four to six thirty with cushy group of 'good' girls
- Not something you do just by virtue of your sex/gender
- Sexual abuse and domestic violence are key issues
- Not too 'agenda-led' e.g. only doing girls work to bring down teenage pregnancy rates…
- …But we do need to be aware of latest agendas and capitalize on them for funding, support and resources?
- Being a bit rebellious
- Celebrating being a woman and multiple identities
- Rights and responsibilities
- How we 'elegantly challenge' people on sexism
- Looking at other more politicized youth work for ideas e.g. LGBT (lesbian, gay, bisexual and trans youth work)
- Knowing that people are unaware of their own oppression, so we need to learn about own oppression and then help others learn
- Subtle sometimes e.g. you wouldn't say 'today we are going to talk about abuse'. You might do mask making to explore identity where issues of abuse may come up
- Feminism – but be careful of when you use the word. You might have to be 'manipulative' so you can make your point but avoid being seen as 'just that feminist one'
- Breaking down stereotypes
- Building on the positive
- A journey from hair and nails sessions onward, if you even begin with these!
- 'Liberation education' – you need to address blocks and barriers and sexism

then use feminism as tool to be free
- Working alongside staff from other services and local councilors
- Addressing part-time workers needs and the needs of volunteers, including training and childcare!
- Moving away from crime and disorder/ controlling young people or all about performance (young women are not just 'targets' we need to meet)
- Helped by training that goes straight to the new and existing clubs, in the places where people work e.g. included in a module of an NVQ/ Diploma, and is accessible to volunteers and training for young people!
- Something useful for those who do boy's youth work and mixed youth work too
- About understanding sexism and 'transphobia' - a fear or hatred of people who are trans. (Trans means people who don't fit the narrow idea of what society says is 'male' and 'female' or who want to change their body/physical expression to fit their inner gender)
- Looking at gender and gender stereotypes – e.g. ride the wave of encouraging women in formal education into science
- Not about hating men – it IS about recognising the injustice for women in society
- Issues in practice – offering safe places and fun activities as a starting point if you want to e.g. beauty session at the start. But then move on and do more e.g. look at history, culture, own family, identity and self awareness, then awareness of people around us
- Not too heavy – you must do the work in bite sized bits, with plenty of fun and joy too!
- Empowering young women. Does this mean disempowering young men? Men's work important to in order to explore this
- Challenging sexism is a key part and must be done with single gender work with young men too
- About challenging a lack of 'politicisation' in young people – Helping young people see that the Personal is Political- we need to bring the politics back!
- Continuously a challenge, but always worth it!

And here are some theories that can help inform youth work practice:

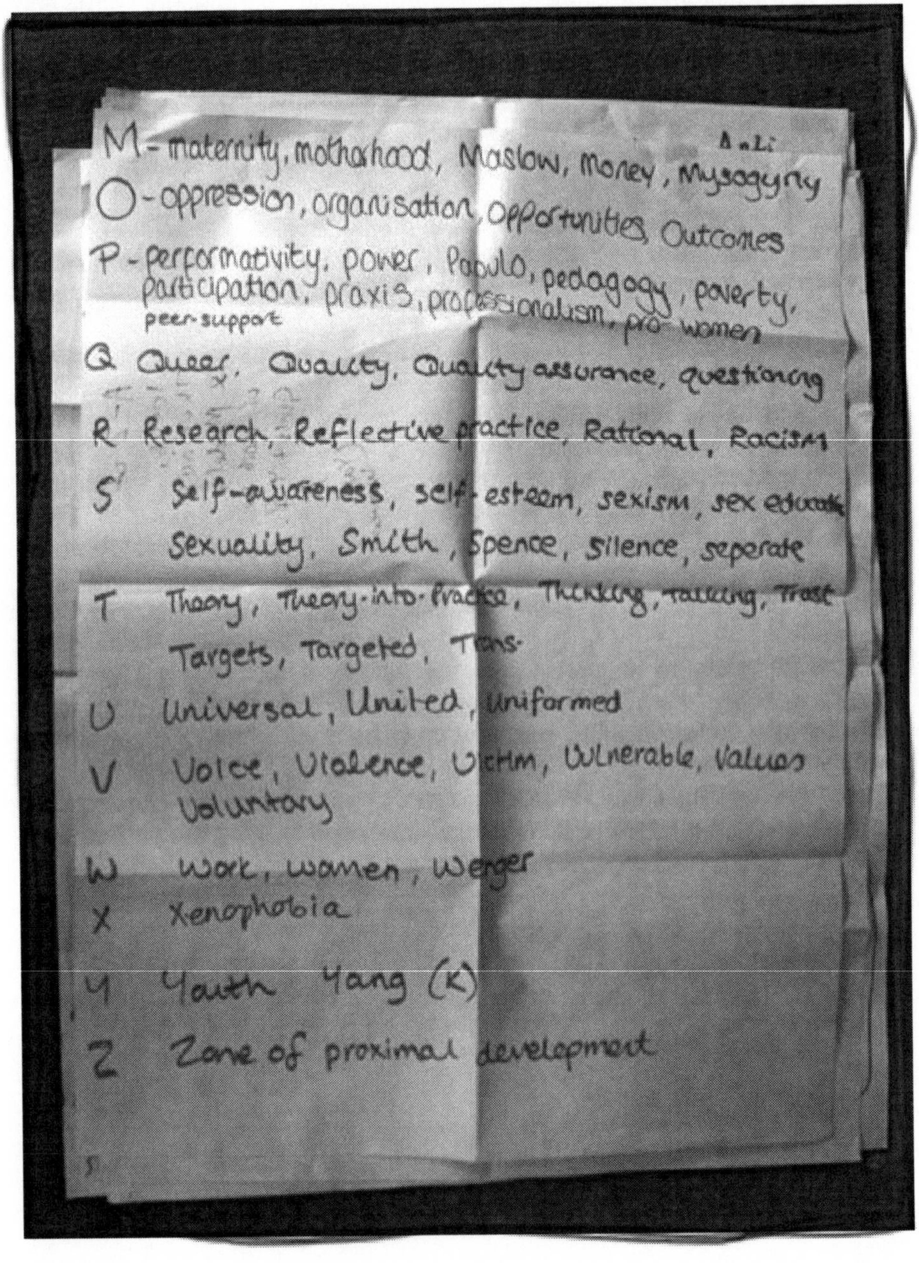

M – maternity, motherhood, Maslow, money, misogyny
O – oppression, organisation, opportunities, outcomes
P – performativity, power, Paulo, pedagogy, poverty, participation, praxis, professionalism, pro-women, peer-support
Q Queer, Quality, Quality assurance, questioning
R Research, Reflective practice, Rational, Racism
S Self-awareness, self-esteem, sexism, sex education, Sexuality, Smith, Spence, silence, separate
T Theory, Theory-into-practice, Thinking, talking, Trust, Targets, Targeted, Trans-
U Universal, United, uniformed
V Voice, Violence, Victim, Vulnerable, Values, Voluntary
W Work, women, Wenger
X Xenophobia
Y Youth, Yang (K)
Z Zone of proximal development

What ideas do you have for youth work with girls and young women?

Why not jot some of them down here : (See if you can make an A-Z!)

If you are interested in setting up or joining a girls work club, either as a volunteer or young person, then have a look online, including on our Feminist Webs website, for where your local groups might be. And do get in touch with us if you want any help.

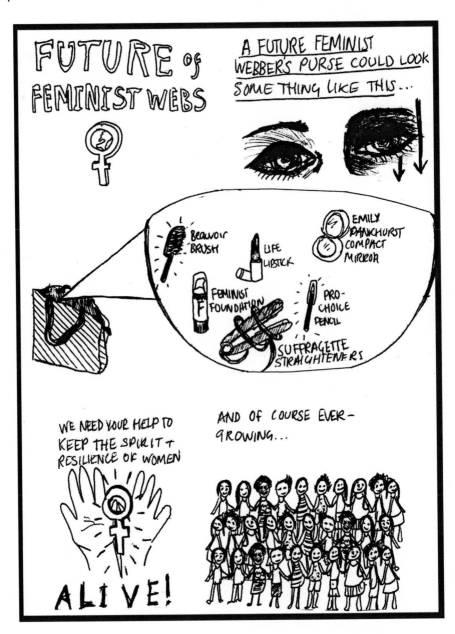

Illustration by Hebe Phillips

Illustration by Hebe Phillips

And finally...

So, dear reader, this brings us to the end of our exciting journey through time and space to bring you joy, hope and inspiration through the delights of feminism and feminist history.

Just remember, the exciting life of being a woman starts with you, today, right now in fact. What will you do with it?

If you want to, write yourself a promise here, or even a plan of action, or perhaps even just a note to yourself or to the next reader of this book!

Thank you for travelling with us!

Resources

Feminist Webs in Summary

Feminist webs provides physical and online 'women and girls work spaces' that act as both an archive and a resource for practitioners, volunteers and young women involved in youth and community work with young women.

Feminist webs bias is toward work which encourages participation and is from a feminist 'rights-based' perspective. At present, Feminist Webs has a focus upon the North West of England although it is aiming to influence wider national agendas, particularly around gender equality in youth work and issues affecting girls and young women.

The archive is both a physical resource, held at Manchester Metropolitan University and an online resource. The website has huge amount of downloadable resources, from session plans to audio interviews.

We also have an extensive list of web-links, books and resources online too that we continuously update. To find out more visit feministwebs.com

"

Feminist Webs is an exciting hub of women who come together to share, explore and develop fantastic opportunities for other women and girls. It brings together people who would not otherwise meet or mix with one another and draws links and connections between them as strong women. It is a delight and a pleasure to be part of something so inspiring. Thank you Fem Webbers!

"

Ali Hanbury

"

I remember your great practice-based and engaging presentation at an otherwise pretty dry feminist academic event!

"

Kim Foale

Contributors

To find out more visit www.feministwebs.com

We would like to thank everyone who has contributed to the book, throught ideas, pictures, articles and events.

Thanks to:

Abi Robertson and **Ruth Ibegbuna** at **Reclaim** for the wo-manifesto www.reclaimproject.org.uk

Ali Hanbury for written contributions, and for being an emerging voice in youth work

Alison Ronan for written contributions and giving birth to Feminist Webs

Alison Steele for being a Feminist Webber in the face of adversity

Amelia Lee for coordinating the Webbers, and editing this book

Caroline Topham, Emily Crompton and **The Spokes** bicycle dance troop for their written and visual contributions

Clare Vermes for oodles of typing, editing and chats

Debi Withers for publishing this book and being our spirit women curator

Divinia Hayes for pioneering the Web down south

Emily Davidson for ideas and quotes

Fi Smith for your artistic contribution and curating the exhibit

Fin Cullen for queering feminisms

Finn Mackay and the **London Feminist Network** for mutual support

Frankie Williams for your ideas and being a North East Feminist Webber

Georgia Rooney for ideas and creating Lesbilicous

Gill Corlett for your artistic contribution with the masks

Harriet Gibson for the Spirit women images

Hebe Phillips for the Feminist Webs Cartoons and Mental Health Cartoon

Hufty for all the web work in the North East and doing super girls' work

Jackie Fleming, for back in 2005 saying to one of our young women, yes, you can use my images and cartoons in your work. You are a legend, thanks! www.jackyfleming.co.uk

Jalna Hanmer and **Sarah** and all at **Feminist Archive North** www.feministarchivenorth.org.uk/about.htm

Janet Batsleer for contributions, genius and constant help

Jayne Mugglestone for being a Feminist Webber

Jean Spence for written contributions, photos and co-birthing Feminist Webs

Jo Adams and Carol Painter for the sexuality flower

Joan Meredith for contributions, and inspiring activism

Jo Lane for written contributions

Julie Tweedale and **Elaine Howard** for bringing us Freedom Personal Safety www.freedompersonalsafety.co.uk

Kim Foale for quotes and challenging conformity

Kimberley Osivwemu for written contributions and quirky thought

Lucy Russell formerly of YWCA, we couldn't find you, but hope you are ok that we included your words and ideas!

Lucy Wright for written contributions and grappling with our feminisms

Maggie Cole for written contributions, being a Feminist Webber and being the grit in the Oyster

Margaret Beetham for written contributions and thoughtfulness

Mary Kenny for written contributions and the Girls Work Network

Milly Shaw for ideas and creating Lesbilicous

Neelam Mehmood for ideas and quotes

Niamh Moore for written contributions, edits and being our pet academic

Omena Osivwemu for written and visual contributions, and inspiration

Rachel Ramchurn for your artistic contribution, clay and sculpting histrees

Razia and the **Brook Manchester volunteers** for creating the speculum-beak ducks

Ruthie Boycott Garnett for your stories, wisdom and work with YWHP

Sally Carr for written contributions and inspiring a generation of youth workers

Sam Aziz and Million Women Rise www.millionwomenrise.com

Sarah Evans for your artistic contribution, and drama with SPY

Sarah Gilston for oodles of typing and conversations

Sarah Greaves for artistic support on the MY BODY banner

Sofia Antonia Milone for images

Stevie Moulton for the Feminist Webs logo

Sue John and **Adele Patrick** and all those at **Glasgow Women's Library** www.womenslibrary.org.uk

Sue Robson for keeping the web alive in the North East and writing about us

Tamzin Forster for all your wonderful art including designing this book www.tamzinforster.co.uk

Teresa Doherty, **Chandan Mahal** and the team at **The Women's Library** www.londonmet.ac.uk/thewomenslibrary

Tracey Gue for our website and beautiful publications

Vanessa Fay for her poetry and being a Feminist Webber

Viv Whitaker for written contributions, positivity and being a Feminist Webber

Contributions from the Brinnington Youth Project by:

Lauren Rowe

Lucie Pollitt

Kate Rapley

Jessica Coups

Demi Williams

Tamara Horton

Yasmin Mohan

Ellie Kennedy

Donna Higgins

Gill Corlett

Nicola Fone

Kizzy Lawton

Gina McCrae

Inge Challinor

Rachael Walker

Contributions from the Halton Young Women's Adventure Club by:

Simone Clarke

Courney Dyas

Kirsty Dyas

Amy Gorry

Terpsihori Karagiannis

Erin Kelly

Jessica Lee

Kimberley Lever

Lisa Lloyd

Chloe Murray

Taylor Reynolds

Amy Clarke

Daisy Nolan

Margi Greaves

Tanya Whitfield

Marie Speed

Sally Carr

Viki Richard

Abbie Potter

Charil Shrimpton

Rochelle Pike

Littler

Irene Johnson

Lesley Jackson

Ann Kingsbury

Kate Ferguson

Keris Keely

Dani Norwood

Sarah Orr

Kerry-Leigh Coombes

Rev. Dawn Harrison

Contributions from the St Peters Youth Project by:

Shazia Begum	Khaushma
Nazia Begum	Aisha Ahmed
Ahida Begum	Safia Zaman
Shahera	Jeni Dale
Alisha Shaw	Mariam Zaman
Betty Gallery	Firdaus Ditta
Sammantha Derbyshire	Ansah Qasim
Lehanne Mahoney	Victoria Clark Leece
Darcie Lamb	Surrya Glover
Ellie Watkins	Abbi Ferati

Contributions from the Young Women's Health Project - LIK:T - by:

Laura Critchley	Sian Ng
Harriet Gibson	Liz Rostron
Hebe Phillips	Natasha Redding-Howe
Heather Davidson	Rachel Blanchard
Meg Nubley	Myrtle Finley
Liz Wilson	Sally Carr
Dr Niamh Moore	Claire Holmes
Ruth Boycott Garnett	Claire Stephan
Esther Ferry-Kennington	Hannah Wood

Sally Carr

Steph Champion

Sophie Lau

Rachel Roantree

Alice Massey

Kelly Parish

Hayleigh Knight

Hazel O'Keefe

Naomi

...And thank you to all the hundreds of young women, older women and those inbetween who have contributed to Feminist Webs since we began.

We would also like to thank the partner organisations and funders that help Feminist Webs to thrive.

Notes

Space for your notes, ideas and thoughts

Lightning Source UK Ltd.
Milton Keynes UK
UKOW051319200412

191164UK00001B/8/P